THE GET REAL GUIDE

TO RETIREMENT

The Balanced, Down-to-Earth Guide

To a Rewarding and Happy Retirement

BY JUDITH C. PAGEL

AND FRANKLIN H. SCHAPIRO

Table of Contents

Preface

Welcome to the *Get Real Guide to Retirement*. In our guide, we are going to attempt to provide a little better balance in our approaches to retirement.

Much of our attention will be centered on the Baby Boom generation, the group now starting to enter retirement and very likely you. It seems that when the topic "Retirement" is attached to the group "Baby Boom," one of two things happens:

• Scenes of idyllic luxury float by – endless hours of golf on a course that makes playing St. Andrews seem pedestrian, travel to remote and more than exotic places, hours with the grandchildren as often as one wishes, antique shopping in that idyllic New England town, etc., etc.

OR

• Dire warnings that Baby Boomers are facing an economic catastrophe in retirement. They have not saved anywhere nearly enough to support themselves. They have squandered away the surplus the Greatest Generation left them. They spent money they did not have. They have left the country in terrible shape. Most will face their senior years in abject poverty, etc., etc.

Do both of those approaches bother you? They should. We really need to "get real" here. Both scenarios have smidgens of truth in them, emphasis on "smidgens". Lots of retirement is lots of fun. And money, of course, is going to be an issue. We do, however, need to put a little perspective on both sides of these issues.

We need to devise the best way to approach our future – the good and the bad. This guide is dedicated to showing us myriads of ways to improve our retirement lot and make sure we are at least heading toward a fun, fantastic retirement.

As two people who have just been through the beginning stages of this life change, we need to tell you that a lot of it is going to be great. There will be mistakes, however. We have found that life is always changing. Life is never really predictable. But we have learned this: whatever mistakes we will make going forward, we will manage to find a way around them.

We can hear you going, "Oh sure – we really believe that one." But stay with us for a moment. Chapter 1 will give you a glimpse of our really big beginning faux pas. We moved to the wrong city. We did our homework. We knew our topic. We judged well. It was a disaster.

But we learned that we can change things. Life, at least for the moment, is now going well. All we had to do was move. Time has passed. Now, when we read Chapter 1, you might even hear a faint giggle as we recall the most outrageous parts.

In our *Get Real Guide* we will try to provide a heads up for some of the possible pitfalls you might face. We will show you how to turn those around. We will also alert you to the coming good times. *(You can figure out how to handle those times yourself.)*

We intend to cover all the bases, from having enough money saved to keeping a happy self to getting along with the medical profession to getting a retirement job to planning on how to live independently to you name it – we will cover it. But best of all, we are also going to cover a lot of issues you will **not** have read about before. The reason is simply that **one has to have been there to have had the experience**. That brings us around to why we think we have something to offer.

About Us

At this point, you are probably asking why we are the authors. The answer is simple. When we started writing, we noticed **that those**

writing about retirement have mostly not been there. Isn't that interesting?

We are both, in fact, retired and we did so relatively recently. Are we Boomers? In truth, my spouse and I are not really Baby Boomers, although we think of ourselves as such. We were, in fact, born two years too soon. **As such, we faced many Boomer problems just about two years *before* the Boomers, and we continue to do that today.**

Our group was the one that went through split sessions in high school – too many kids for the space, so half of us went from 7 a.m. to noon and the other half went from noon to 5 p.m. By the time we graduated, they were building the new schools for the Boomers. We graduated just in time to find out that jobs were really getting scarce because, again, there were too many Boomers. Finally, we have been in retirement a few years now and as we noted above, we have already faced many of the problems you will face. We know what you are going to face before you face it.

As we said, we have made some mistakes that, hopefully, we can help you avoid. We also have listened carefully to our retired friends – not to do an impersonal interview, but to hear what they are really thinking about. And we happily share with you all we have learned.

Additionally, we bring relevant areas of expertise to the table beyond being born at the right time. As his last job, Frank held a position in wealth management and asset allocation at one of the nation's largest banks, giving him valuable financial background. Judy, whose last job was as an IT project manager, has recently had to get used to having a long-term disability, giving her premature insight into what more advanced years may bring. We both are big data, high tech doctorates, so we tend to put emphasis on information from well-designed, randomly controlled studies, but we also loved our years of teaching and we pride ourselves on making sure that everyone understands, no matter how complicated or strange the material.

About the Guide

Now, about our Guide: This book is specifically for those of you who are considering retiring within ten years and those who are in their first ten years of retirement. This version of the Guide is directed to those of you who, for the most part, are still in fairly good shape (mentally and physically, at least on your terms) and who are interested in making the most of your retirement days. Our main goal is to help you be able to enjoy your retirement and, more importantly, to continue to enjoy it for many years.

One more point: Retirement is not a point in time. It is a process. Things will change. Continuous adjustments will have to be made. We will provide help in managing that change and provide suggestions for how best to handle the adjustments.

A major theme you will see underlying the entire guide is that retirement, just like the life we have already led, is unpredictable. These days things are really unpredictable and lots of change will be as omnipresent as your future aches and pains. Those pictures at the beach, on the golf course, in the river, are little points in time. Surrounding those points is a full life – full of positives and negatives that make us real people. Here's to that life!

Finally, the Guide was written with the thought of avoiding ponderous prose in favor of easy reading. Just take it easy, and see if any of the suggestions might be of use for you.

We are going to take you through many of the decisions you will face, in approximate chronological order. We will start with the decision of whether to stay in your home or move to that retirement mecca. We will move from there to how much you will need to save and how you can keep healthy with a vibrant mind. We will end up with suggestions for everyday living, including tons of activities to keep you happy and moving, as well as a guide to making a super job in retirement. We have also included an extensive bibliography to help you explore these topics further.

Again, welcome to our Guide. May it provide you with at least one or two suggestions you like.

Judith C. Pagel and Franklin H. Schapiro

Chapter 1: Stay in Your Home or Move

In Our Dreams

One of the very first decisions about your retirement that you will make is whether to stay in your home city or move to another town. Staying has a lot of advantages. Moving has a lot of advantages.

Staying in your home city has many, many advantages. For many, the main advantage is a support group of persons who have known you for years and who would not think twice of offering to get you to the doctor or to sit with you when you need a friend or someone with whom to have those really good times. This might become critical should you be left on your own at some point. Also, staying put will allow many of you to watch the grandkids grow up and go to their ballgames and dance recitals. (One retiree we have heard about reports that the kids were so upset at his plans for moving that he stored all the family furniture and goods for a year, so he could change his mind.)

On the other hand, there is also something so very appealing about the idea of spending the rest of your days lounging under the southern sun in Palm Beach or Palm Springs or Miami or Phoenix, etc., etc. Alternatively, a lot of us are drawn to the quintessential New England life with that beautiful church steeple right in the middle of town and those incredible fall colors and antiquing as you stroll through those friendly small towns. And then there is always the call of the wild and those mountains – either to a quiet mountain retreat near a stream and hidden in the back woods near Cheshire or Asheville in North Carolina or the mountains of the West and hiking with snow-covered peaks over your shoulder. Or you may dream about lazily cycling to those incredibly delightful, unique shops in

Reed, Oregon. Or finally, you may move simply to be closer to the kids and grandkids.

Get Real Time

But here comes our warning. We confess – early on we were attracted to a location like one of those dream meccas above. The area had a particularly legendary quality. We moved there as our first step in retirement and heard from a lot of envious friends, who would have loved to have a part of our dream.

But sometimes things do not work out when one moves to a new city or town. You may miss the kids. You may miss friends of very long standing. You may feel isolated, but also, you may just fail to connect in the new town. We truly failed to connect and, at the risk of being seen as overly negative, we think we should warn you about that.

However, before we do, let us reassure you that we have now moved to a new town less than an hour away. We have been very impressed with our new home. We really like it here. First, there is a vibrant Senior Center and also a really active Newcomer's club. Organizations in the town want new members and put notices in the newspaper, especially the ones that require a sponsor like the Rotary and Lions clubs. People here are anxious to meet new friends. Stranger conversations at the grocery store or drug store or big box are very frequent and very pleasant. Within a few weeks of living here, three restaurants knew us by name. Both young and old are very considerate of age and disabilities and offer help on a moment's notice. One warning: don't park in the handicapped spot unless you are entitled, because someone will take you up on your impolite behavior, in front of everybody. ADA compliant housing is easy to find. The town is very proud of their new park, which is a beautiful example of Universal Design, so that everyone regardless of any disabilities can enjoy themselves. And yes, our four-footed furry friends have their own park section and swimming pond which they truly enjoy. Finally, everyone is happy to give you recommendations for whatever and to help you settle in.

However, back to our first retirement choice: Those of you familiar with the Chevy Chase film, *Funny Farm*, will remember that the welcoming for Chevy and his wife was less than hospitable. A lot less. Tons less. Well, it happened to us. There were times we thought we must have some form of the plague. It was clear: **These people just did not want us in their town.** They did not go quite so far as a showdown at sunset, but it was close – very close. We spent many days trying to figure out why we did not see this situation coming.

While we still do not fully understand, we do have a sage bit of advice for our readers: **Test out the new town as best you can before you move.** Do what you can to feel out that new town you are thinking of calling your own. Get a subscription to the newspaper. Spend some time people watching. If possible, spend some time with people you already know who live there. There can't be too many cities like our first choice, but as Grandma, or someone, used to say, "Better safe than sorry." Yes, we did make a mistake in our first city choice, but it was a relatively easy mistake to undo.

Solutions

Identifying Not So Friendly Towns

Watch out for the following: These situations *actually happened* either to us or to others upon moving to one or more of what we are going to call *NotSoFriendly Towns*:

- **You become invisible.**

  Perhaps the single best description we found for our situation was from another couple who also had not reacted well to the same NotSoFriendly Town to which we first moved. The couple said when they moved there, they simply became invisible. People walked around them as if they were not there.

Strange, they frequently referred to their new home as Stepford.

This may be hard to judge before you move, but we can tell you that in our new town people tend to talk to strangers, so you are bound to start some kind of little conversation in the mall, the store, wherever. Watch for the lack of little stranger conversations on your shopping trip in the new town. (People in *NotSoFriendly Towns* only talk to ones they know.) As an aside, before moving we had noticed a good deal of bullying by teens at the local mall – much more than we had seen other places. This was a stop sign we clearly missed.

- **To repeat, you become invisible.**

Upon the first visit to a club you are thinking of joining, note the behavior of the members when the meeting is over. One newcomer to a NotSoFriendly Town we know was waiting outside for her spouse to pick her up. Other members leaving the meeting had to pass by her to get to the parking lot. None stopped to 1) say how nice it was to meet her, 2) ask if she was OK, 3) ask if she needed a ride, or 4) hit her up for a twenty. Yes, invisible.

- **Your disabilities are your problem (and alas, also your personal failing).**

An example of this is best seen at the entrance to a restaurant. Watch the disabled lady deftly maneuver her walker, pulling it back while opening the restaurant door. Then see three physically fit strangers take advantage of the open door and enter the restaurant with the disabled one acting as doorman. (We honestly saw this happen, and it occurred repeatedly.) In contrast, in our new town, we have seen people get up and walk 20 feet to the restaurant door in order to offer help to the person with the walker.

- **Stairs for everyone.**

  Remember that you are thinking of retiring. Look carefully to see how many ADA (Americans with Disabilities Act) compliant houses and apartments are available. **Watch out for the all too common dwelling with three steps up to the front door and lots of stairs to the lower level where the washing machine and dryer reside.** This is a good indication of how accepting the locals are to retirees from outside.

- **Breathing not allowed.**

  Listen up for reactions to others. In *NotSoFriendly Town*, one of the members of a club we might have joined was overheard complaining about a couple of older members who "had the nerve to roll their oxygen tanks into the meeting."

- **Secret meetings.**

  Try watching the newspaper for meeting times for national organizations that tend to occur in most cities – like Lions, Rotary, etc. See if any of the organizations show an interest in new members. See if any advertise when their next meeting will occur. (Most of these organizations require a new member to be sponsored by an existing one. However, if someone new to town cannot find out anything about these clubs or get to know anyone who belongs, they also will not be able to find a sponsor. We found this in *NotSoFriendly Town*, allowing us to refer to it as *The World's Largest Gated Community* – and newcomers will kindly remain outside the gates.)

- **The interrogation.**

  When introduced to new townspeople, is what follows similar to what one might call *an interrogation?* If they want to know how long you were breastfed and whether you ever had detention in the third grade, you are in *NotSoFriendly Town*.

- **Old friends – well, maybe not.**

  On one of your trips, put together a lunch of friends and people you already know in *NotSoFriendly Town*. Note if you are left doing all the organizing and see if anyone calls afterward. Keep track to see if any of *NotSoFriendly's* residents offer an invite to dinner after you arrive.

- **You are on your own.**

  When trouble arises – say that one of you lands in the hospital – see how many "friends" show at the hospital.

- **Need a plumber – you are still on your own.**

  You have moved to this new town and, sooner or sooner, you are going to need some kind of household help. Everyone in town raves about the brothers of a certain family who do everyone's lawn work. Now, try to get one of the townsfolk to give you the brothers' phone number. It will not happen. *(This was truly one of the hallmarks of our NotSoFriendly Town. We never did understand why it was impossible to get a recommendation – any recommendation.)*

- **You are only a good customer of mine if we went to high school together.**

  Note that above we talked about locals only speaking to those they know. That is also frequently someone who went to the same high school. On the other hand, as a newcomer, you can visit an establishment hundreds of times and the manager will never know who you are. (In contrast, in our new town, six weeks in there were three restaurants where they already knew our name.)

Finding Friendly Towns

As a final step, let us provide you with the one trait that might tell you that you are not moving to *Stepford, NotSoFriendly Town,* or *the World's Largest Gated Community*. Besides noting a willingness to talk to strangers, do look for a bit a humor seen in life, and most especially, self-effacing humor. When one realizes that one is not perfect and one can still laugh about it, then one has room for newcomers and new friends, who also may not be perfect.

We watched George Clooney on the David Letterman show the other night. He had one funny line after another. We also learned where that sense of humor came from, because George's dad and mom were in the Green Room. David asked George's dad if he had ever worked in Dayton. Dad looked up and with a perfectly straight face said, "I have been fired from most of the major cities in the United States." For a person with such a distinguished career as George's dad, it was truly refreshing and assured you that you could live in a place with people like that.

Chapter 2: Where to Move and Whether to Rent or Buy

In Our Dreams

While some of you plan on remaining in your family home, a recent study from Better Homes and Gardens Real Estate reports that the majority of Baby Boomers (57%) say they are planning to move to a new home in retirement (Hannon, 2014). As such, the key question for many of you is going to be *where*. (We are assuming that Chapter 1 convinced you to take our advice and avoid a *NotSoFriendly Town*, but that only leaves a few thousand options after that.)

Each of us has our own picture of their ideal retirement setting. For some it is that small rural town where life moves at a glacier's slow pace, but happily. For others, the lure of big city living with all of its exciting activities wins out. And, of course, in between these two lie endless possibilities.

So how do you choose among the rural towns or among the big metros or among those in the middle? You have probably considered towns on those "Ten Best Places to Retire" lists, or better yet, the "Ten Least Expensive Places to Retire."

Get Real Time

As you get close to decision time, we would like to suggest a little "Get Real" activity to go along with your "Top 10 List" reading. To provide guidance, we strongly recommend putting together a preliminary budget for living in a town or two at the top of your current wish lists. (Local government offices and apartment staffs or real estate agents should be able to help with estimated costs for water, sewer, gas, and electric.)

This activity may be much more important than first thought, as we have been learning that areas frequently listed on those "Ten Least Expensive Places to Retire" lists may not be as inexpensive as advertised. We are hearing that states with no income tax may also *not* be the cheapest places to live with all costs in, particularly utilities. Do check out the utilities and local sales taxes, as this is where you will see differences that can *wipe out the no income tax advantage*. This will not always be true, but it is good to check.

Solutions

Preparing a Preliminary Budget

Below is a comparison of two *actual* budgets from one to two years ago for a recently retired couple. The "No State Income Tax" column contains figures from a state with no personal income tax. The "State Income Tax" column contains figures from a town about three times the size of the first. This state does have a personal income tax.

The figures are for 12 months. They are for the same retired couple, who lived in both towns. In both cases, the retired couple rented, rather than purchased. In the No Tax state, they rented a house. In the Tax state, they rented an apartment in a large complex with a pool and fitness center. Also included in the rent for the apartment was a garage with a very large amount of storage space.

Preliminary Budget	No State Income Tax	State Income Tax
Monthly Rent (1)	$13,536	$16,704
Storage	540	0
Renter's Insurance	197	214
Gas & Electricity	2,416	841
Water, Sewer, & Trash	1,519	510
Maintenance & Yard	855	125
Other Services (2)	830	0
Auto License Fees/Taxes	245	187
Auto Maintain/Repair (3)	782	473
Gasoline Costs (4)	1,474	1,482
State Income Tax	0	1,689
Total Annual	**22,394**	**22,225**

(1) Includes an Amortized Security Deposit plus storage expenses.

(2) A Fitness Center Package was included in the rent at the Income Tax State apartment.

(3) Included regular maintenance plus road wear items (tires, lights, etc.).

(4) Calculated on an equal miles basis.

Notes about Expenses

1. First, make sure you are including all relevant budget items.
Some are not instantly obvious. As retirees we have lived in both a state with relatively high taxes, as well as one with very low taxes.

Further, we have friends who have retired in both a high and low tax state. Of note, we both have the same basic story. Be very careful about the following when budgeting:

- **Do check out utility fees in general, but especially utility minimums.**

> In the low tax state with which we are familiar, both the utility rates and the utility minimums were high. Simply turning on all of the utilities incurred a minimum bill in excess of $200 per month. In the higher tax state, the minimum bill was less than $15. Our friends found a similar situation in another low tax state.

- **Insurance rates (either home-owner or rental) can vary widely depending on police, fire, and so on.**

> Motor vehicle costs can also vary widely.

- **Do include the services which are provided at the rental or with the property you are considering buying, such as green fees, swimming pools, etc.**

> (What fees are charged, what discounts are offered, and how available are the services?)

2. Remember that there are really no free lunches.

In low tax states, the money to support public functions has to come from somewhere – hidden fees, license fees, car registration fees, etc. We and our friends learned the hard way that low taxes and low cost are not necessarily synonymous. In our case the low income tax state turned out to be the state with the higher living expenses.

3. Finally, an expense that many of you will need to allow for is *storage*.

Over time we have reduced our storage needs, but moving from bigger to smaller is likely to create the need for storage lockers, sheds, etc. Perfect planning and weeding out and selling off is a great goal, but (time to get real), getting rid of some of those tools or grandma's cup collection is harder than you think. And we really do know this one from experience.

Whether to Rent or Buy

There is one other very important decision you will need to make. Regardless of whether you choose to stay in your home town or find a new berg, unless you decide to remain in the family home, your next decision will probably be whether to rent or buy. Let us start with one piece of advice. **If at all possible, rent for a while if this is a new town.** Actually, for anyone moving to a completely new place – not simply retirees – renting is probably good advice, so you get to know a little about the area.

In Chapter 1, we introduced you to a very small number of towns who will not be overjoyed to see you come. However, even among the thousands and thousands of very nice towns, there will also be very real problems of getting to the new place and then realizing that you really miss your old friends or your children or even things to do and places to go you really liked. We understand that a number of small city folk move to the big city and do not like the traffic. We understand that a number of big city folk move to a smaller city and miss the amenities of the big city. We understand that a number of northerners move to the south and then realize they are not fit for hot summers in the sun. We understand that a number of southerners move to the north and then realize they are not fit for shoveling 12 feet of snow each winter. Renting will save your finances from what these days might be a lengthy attempt to sell the *new* home, so you can move on or move back.

Finally, had we written this book ten years ago, I am pretty sure the advice would have been to buy. Even today, if the rate is low (3.5% flat rate and you intend to be there for at least 7 years), buying may be a good financial decision. (Please note that by now most mortgages are already above 3.5 %.)

1. Regardless, the one action you do want to take is to make a preliminary budget to compare renting versus buying.

Since the Great Recession, all of us have had to reconsider, if only for a moment, whether buying a family home is, in fact, always the best way to go. These days, each city needs to be considered separately. Changes in pricing and mortgage rates need to be followed religiously. While we compared two rental properties above, we also humbly suggest a direct comparison between buying and renting in each town being considered. There are two other factors to be considered:

2. If you purchase a home, there will be some kind of down payment.

That down payment will use up some amount of your retirement savings. As such, that will leave you with less money to carry you through retirement. You need to determine how that will affect future withdrawals from your now reduced savings.

3. Finally, you will get a deduction for the property tax on your taxes, but it may be less important to you as a retiree.

It may be less important because you may be making less and the income tax rate will therefore be less. Note that a $10,000 property tax deduction will be worth $2800 if you are in the 28% bracket (making $146,000-223,000), but only $1500 if you are in the 15% bracket (making $18,000-72,000) (Daugherty, 2013).

Chapter 3: Retire Early, On Time, Or Later

In Our Dreams

Haven't we all, at one time or another, dreamt of those idyllic days of retirement – a quiet day fishing at your favorite fishing hole with the sun sparkling through the icy cold water and reflecting off that humongous fish you are about to catch – walking out onto the golf course a few feet from the front door with the early morning sun shimmering through the mist onto the green – hiking to the top of the mountain just in time to see the tequila sunrise sky streaking across the horizon – spring time with the grand children teaching them the finer points of throwing a baseball – cuddling up in a big, cushy chair with, finally, time to read, etc., etc.

The setting may be a little different for each of us, but the dream is still there and – importantly – retirement in the dream is always early enough so we are all healthy enough to really enjoy it. Fifty-five seems to be a magic age chosen by a lot of us. *(OK, there are some who say they want to work forever and would not know what to do with the spare time – but then, they most likely did not buy this book.)*

Get Real Time

This guide is really all about *the best laid plans oft going awry*. But never fear, we will tell you how to cope and thrive at the same time. *Honest, retirement often does come through on the dream, and when it does, it does so ten times over. We speak from experience.* But first, let us look at some of those dreams without the rose-colored glasses, i.e., "get real time."

Now, some folks do retire at 55 or in their early 60's. One reason for many is that they were laid off somewhere during that time and were not able, at their "advanced" age, to get the next job, or at least one that fits their skills. This is "get real time."

You have no idea the strength of age discrimination until you try to find your next job in your early 60's. Reasons for not hiring you go on and on and on. After all, you do not have the energy. You will not be able to work for a younger boss. You will not be able to work for a woman. You do not understand the younger workers and will not be able to become a good "member of the team." *(This is a frequently used excuse. No wonder that the tendency is to flee from any job interview where the interviewers are still on their first job or young enough to be dating your grandkids.)* You will not be able to work for any boss. You do not need the job and thus will leave shortly after taking it. Most important, you will require a high salary, reason enough to get rid of you from the last job and not hire you for the next. Even if you do not *require* more money, they will think you do – the ultimate Catch 22.

Solutions

You Will Know When

Actually, there are many factors determining when to enter retirement, and not all are under one's control. But if retirement comes from a lost job or a blocked career, all is not lost. It is not impossible to get a good job in your 60's, but you will need patience, and lots of it. *(We know firsthand.)* Or, alternatively, you can start your own business. *(We will provide ideas.)* Or alternatively, you can find other sources of income. *(We will provide examples.)* On the not so good side – you may wish to work until you reach 70, but your body – or your spouse's – may be telling you that that scenario in not going to be in the stars. You may want to or need to retire now.

Truth is, there are two major factors that can limit retirement decisions. The first is money. The second is your or another family member's health. Both will tell you when the time is appropriate. And we will be here to help you along.

About Finding That Job Before and During Retirement

The next few chapters are going to investigate how much money we will need for retirement, some of the reasons why Boomers have had an especially hard time putting together a sufficient nest egg, and how we can make up the difference between what we have and what we need.

Many of you, however, are already asking about – are getting really antsy about – working through retirement. **To those of you who think you will be working for some time due to a savings shortfall, the last chapter of our Guide will seriously address getting – or making – that job**. Relax. As we get further into the 21st century, we are finding that whole new worlds are opening up.

Opportunities are available that would not have been conceived of a decade ago. Think for a minute. Were we using the camera on our mobile phone to deposit a check in the 1990's? No. Were we carrying around a small pad which connected us to the internet whenever we wanted? No. Did a driverless car just pass by our door, mapping stop signs? No. Think what could happen before 2020.

Yes, the world has changed immensely and will change in many ways which can help us get that job in retirement. For example, we now have "crowdfunding" as a way to gather money for our entrepreneurial efforts, including sites such as kickstarter.com. *(Kickstarter claims to be the largest funding platform for creative projects in the world.)* We have large corporations making fortunes for their founders such as Twitter who, as we write this, still does not have a large source of income. We now have the ability to carry out many business activities easily on our own, such as designing a company website, designing our own business cards and logos, shipping goods easily, etc., etc. All in all, it is easier to start a company now than it ever has been. We will provide lots of ideas for you.

But first, let us examine those money issues.

Chapter 4: How Much Do We Need to Save?

In our Dreams

In order to calculate how much we need to save for a solid retire-ment, let us look first at the savings recommended by the financial planners whose articles we keep seeing. While there are many differ-ent approaches to retirement savings, the approach below tends to be straight forward and is currently most popular.

Ideally, your savings and other sources of retirement income should produce at least 70% of your pre-retirement income. *(See the websites in the Bibliography, Chapter 4, from StateFarm, CNN-Money, and The Department of Labor.)* For example, in 2012, the median household income for those 55-64 according to the Census Bureau was slightly under $60,000. If you made $60,000 pre-retirement, you can probably live nicely in retirement with $42,000 per year in income. (Note that job related costs, such as transporta-tion costs and a clothing budget, largely disappear.)

In addition, the most common advice is that you can plan to take out 4% per year from your savings (Waggoner, 2013). Taking out 4% should ensure that you will not outlive your savings.

Example: Let us say a couple needs $42,000. Both worked steadily throughout their working lives, and they have checked their accounts and are expecting about $32,500 a year from social security – $16,250 apiece. Thus, savings need to cover $42,000 minus $32,500 = $9500. (We did a bit of rounding here, to make calculations easier.)

(Come up with the equation below by simply saying that "$9500 is (=) 4% (.04) of (*) what you will need (X)."

We are trying to find out how much we will need, so call it
X, and solve the equation.)
$$9500 = .04 * X$$
$$X = 9500/.04$$
$$X = \$237,500$$

You will need \$237,500 in savings in order to provide the *desired* \$42,000 in retirement income. Now, 4% seems a bit small. After all, a person saves nearly a quarter million dollars and only gets \$9500 per year, or close to \$800 per month, to live on. That is really chintzy!

The 4% actually comes from studies that have looked historically at how much interest was made yearly over some period of time like 30 years (a somewhat typical retirement timeframe) from a portfolio of stocks and bonds set up conservatively for retirement. The studies found that if you take out 4% a year, you should not outlive your money. (The assumption here is that over many years the retirement fund will make on average at least 4% each year in interest to replace what you take out each year.)

One last note on how much to save and even easier to remember: using the equation above, you can solve to find that, for each \$1000 per year you will need in income (beyond social security), you will need to save \$25,000. (Replace the \$9500 in the equation with \$1000 and solve.)

Is 4% Really Going to Get Us Through Retirement?
The studies that yielded 4% as a reasonable value for what to take each year from retirement funds were studies carried out when the average interest rate was running around 8%. Unfortunately, as any recent retiree will tell you, the interest rate has varied recently between 1% and 2%. The question is whether such a low rate will produce enough interest income to keep the retirement fund going for as long as we need. There are really two answers to this question. First, the 4 % value was selected to be conservative. Second, very few ex-

pect interest rates to stay quite so low for an extended period of time in our future. Rates are expected to go up and that will produce more interest income to keep the retirement fund going. But a word of caution: the expectation that rates would start back up soon has been with us for a while and they have not.

Of course, we really don't know and can't tell, but the recent very low rates have been seen so rarely in our past that we do have at least some reason to believe that they won't stay this low for too long. If they do, everyone is going to have to make adjustments and our retirement funds will be only a very small part of that.

One last point: related to these issues is the question of whether you intend to leave some part of that retirement fund to your children. As we said above, the reason we can keep our accounts going for such a long time – often 30 years or even more – is that, even though each year we take money out (say 4%), after that we put money back in from the interest that the account makes each year. If the interest the account makes is at least 4% on average, then theoretically, the fund should remain stable over the years except for fees, taxes, etc., that will lower the fund amount. What is left would be there for the children's or others' inheritance.

An aside: please note the phrase above "except for fees, taxes." Be very aware of *fees*. It is not surprising to see that fees can have a very strong impact on capital appreciation. Be vigilant for "tax sensitive" investments that tend to carry larger total fees which offset some or all of their tax advantages. Depending on your situation, it may be worth talking with a tax specialist in addition to a financial advisor.

Some retirees do not have children or have decided not to leave an inheritance or have decided to provide the inheritance through trusts, etc., before they die. If one is in a position to tap into their principle, a version of the 4% rule can be used. According to many economists, all you need to do is withdraw 4 percent of your nest egg the first year of retirement and then increase that dollar amount each year by the rate of inflation. This will maintain your purchasing power and will give you a 90 percent assurance that your savings will last at least thirty years (Lynott, 2014).

Get Real Time

Now, looking brightly on the world, how much does the average 55+ American have in their 401(k)? As of December, 2013, the amount was $165,200 for those about ready to retire (up from $143,300 in 2012). Oops!! Using the 4% rule will return around $6,600 per year, only about 70% of what the typical family night need.

Now, before you all join the lemming parade, calm down. We have not included other retirement sources of income beyond the 401(k), and especially the value of the family home. As of 2012, the Federal Research Survey found the median family net worth (including the family home) among those 55-64 is $179,400. (Median net worth is total value of assets including the family home minus the value of liabilities, such as college or credit card debt or mortgage.) The median net worth is still short of desired using the 4% rule, but it is much closer. Further, those whose retirement is not immediately imminent will have some time to make up some of the difference.

To give you a feel for how these numbers affect income, the median income among those 55-64 is $58,626 (which drops down to $42,343 among those 65-74).

OK, now we know why the family home is so important. And so exasperating! In 2010, due to the Great Recession and the bursting of the housing bubble, median net worth for *all* adults dropped to $77,300, from $126,400 in 2007, three years earlier. A good part of that drop was due to the drop in home prices, as well as to the drop in stock prices. We are slowly coming out of the Recession, but few Americans will ever put all their faith in home-buying the way they did at the beginning of the 21st century.

Other Numbers You Have Seen

We can see some questioning looks out there. You are asking, "Why do your numbers not match that magic one million dollars or 1.5 million dollars I keep seeing in all the ads?"

The answer here is fairly simple. If you have one million dollars in retirement savings, you can plan, using the 4% rule, to take out $40,000 a year to live on. If you have 1.5 million dollars, you can take out $60,000. Now add around $31,200 from social security *($1294 is the current average monthly benefit in the U.S. times 12 months times 2 workers)*, and you will be living on either $71,200 or $91,200. Remember that you want to make 70% of your pre-retirement salary. Thus, we can say that the $71,200 or $91,200 should be 70% of what these people made pre-retirement. If we do the math, we are referring to folks who made $101,714 or $130,285 before retirement. We can guess that the reason these figures show up so often is because the folks making over $100,000 are precisely those the financial planners would like as clients.

One other issue may have bothered you. You have probably seen many articles bemoaning the fact that Americans have less than $80,000 to $90,000 in their 401(k) accounts. *(Right after the end of the Great Recession, the amounts they quoted were less than $50,000. Fortunately, that amount has grown as we have come out of the recession.)* The figures vary but they're usually under $90,000. That number refers to all Americans, not Americans getting ready to retire. And it just makes sense that the younger members of our society have just begun saving for retirement.

Solutions

We are going to look at various ways of getting more money for the retirement fund. We will divide the options into two parts: those using equity in a family home (including a single family house, condo, and other dwelling types) and those options from sources not involving equity in a piece of real estate. The one thing you will notice is that there are quite a few different ways in which the home equity can be used to supplement the retirement fund. Do take a good look. In addition, the section not involving real estate can be of value to everyone who wants to supplement their fund.

Options for More Retirement Income Using the Family Home
Even taking into account the price instability shown in the Great Recession, the family home still provides the basis for what many experts consider the safest and best way to retire, given that the mortgage is paid off and the only expenses required are items like home maintenance, home insurance, and taxes. Without having to pay a mortgage or rent means that you can live well on substantially less than 70% of what you made when you worked. So, number 1 on our list of options for more income in retirement is:

1. Live in the fully paid off family home, saving rent or a new mortgage.
Staying in the family home was a major factor in many households that allowed our parents and grandparents to do so well in retirement. Many had paid off their mortgage, so they lived without rent or mortgage, thus saving lots of money.

With her defined benefit pension and social security, my mom made more in retirement than she did working. In addition, she lived out her life in the fully paid off family home, with no mortgage or rent to pay. Not bad. *(Her income allowed several European trips.)*

While this option has many advantages, the option is not available and/or not a good idea in many circumstances. Not all homes are suitable for retiring in place. For example, homes built in the 60's often have very narrow doorways that will not take a walker, scooter, or wheelchair. Room for these items may not seem important when one is in their early sixties, but when and if it does become important, it will be of key importance in the decision-making. Widening doorways is *really* expensive.

Also expensive is adding bathrooms or making changes to bathrooms to make them more accessible. Two additional issues about retiring in place involve maintenance and updating. How likely is your home to deteriorate in ways that may prove expensive? One example is deterioration of the windows: A little leak can be OK, but that leak can cease to be OK if it affects the heating and cooling bill. Like doorway widening, window replacement can be quite expensive.

There are other ways to make use of home equity. The big problem is that what one really wants to do is take out the value of the house at the same time one is using its value by living in it. It is like having one's cake and eating it too. It did not work out real well for Marie Antoinette, but we actually have a solution that can work out here if handled with care.

2. Take out a reverse mortgage.

With a reverse mortgage, you live in your house, you still own the house, you still pay for maintenance, insurance, and taxes, but you also have the equivalent of a home equity line on the house which can be used for any desired purpose. You may use the home equity you already have in the house to pay the mortgage on the part you do not own yet. You may use it to pay off credit cards, college debt, normal living expenses, etc. The rule is that the whole thing becomes due when the last owner moves out of the house.

Caveat: One caveat, before doing a reverse mortgage, is to make sure *exactly* how one works in your area. This means getting advice from somebody who does not stand to gain from your decision, such as an attorney hired by you.

You will find advice that both spouses need to be listed on the title. Otherwise, when one spouse moves say to a nursing home, the reverse mortgage becomes due in full and is usually paid for by selling the house, leaving the remaining spouse with no place to live *and* no money to live on because much or all of the sale proceeds will go to the mortgage holder.

That caveat is only one of many cautions regarding reverse mortgages. Do not take anything said here as the way your reverse mortgage may work. Double check every aspect of the loan. (A loan is what a reverse mortgage really is.)

To reiterate, if you have a good lawyer watch over your taking out the reverse mortgage and you fully understand the terms (like still having to pay all property taxes and having to keep the house in good maintenance) and if you understand that these are enforced and if you don't pay those taxes, your home can be foreclosed upon, then a reverse mortgage may be a reasonable approach to filling out the retirement coffers.

Caveat Two: Our second caveat refers to the fact that the amount available to lend in a reverse mortgage will be smaller than many might expect. Because the rules are so complicated in this area, you will find it difficult to get a good estimate for the amount for which you may qualify. The amount will depend on the amount of equity in the home, the borrower's age, the appraised home value, the going mortgage interest rate, and other variables. However, when we found examples, we were surprised to find that the amount to be borrowed tended to be half or less of the equity in the home.

Before we provide examples, keep in mind that a good proportion of what is left in equity *after* the loan will be owed in interest and fees for that loan. What this means is that little may be left for any heirs.

• The Journal of Accountancy (2006) provides an example of a home worth $300,000 in equity with no debt yielding an available loan principle limit of $142,749 after the initial fees, mortgage insurance, closing costs, etc.

(Note: The monthly adjustable HECM (Home Equity Conversion Mortgage) will pay the owners $1,187.42 for as

long as either of them lives in the home. However, note that after ten years, their accumulated costs (i.e., loan interest plus fees) will equal just over $81,000. That is on top of the $142,000 paid to the owners as part of the loan.)

• **An example from Bloomberg (Leondis, 2008) is for a 70-year-old in New York with a house worth $500,000. He may qualify for a loan as much as $240,000 with $17,000 in fees, including mortgage insurance. In addition, the interest rate for the loan will start at 4%.**

• **The Investor Solutions website (n.d.) gives the example of a 70-year-old single woman with a home valued at $300,000 who might receive a lump sum or line of credit of $122,180, or monthly payments for life of $809.**

You may want to keep in mind the following: 1) These are expensive loans, 2) They are best when the homeowners are older, and 3) Expect little in remaining equity for your heirs.

Finally, for *some* mortgages, if your heirs fully pay off the credit line on your death, they should be able to keep the family home. (However, do be aware that the amount owed will include a substantial amount of interest, and we mean substantial.)

Other sources of additional income for retirement connected with the house and its value are:

3. Sell the current family home and purchase a smaller, less expensive home.

Your new home may be either in the same city or in a city with a lower cost of living. There are a lot of issues involved with selling the current family home. One is your kids, some of whom will no doubt suggest that they were planning on living in the family home at some point. A second issue is simply that the kids will no longer have that place to gather for Christmas/Hanukah and other family occasions. But that is not the real rub.

The real rub has to do with the part about a *smaller/less expensive* house. Again, if you have kids, it may really mean that there is no place for the kids and their families to *stay* for those scrapbook-making holidays. Even if you do not have kids, it still means that friends cannot drop in from across the country and have a nice (free) place to stay.

What you can do is apologize ahead of time and tell everyone that you just no longer have a place for them to stay. *(Some will take it better than others, but remember that this is your life – not theirs. Maybe one of the kids will offer to keep folks for the holidays. On the very pleasant side, we actually had a dear friend who kidded us because we felt we had to let them know there was no place to stay. They hadn't even considered it.)*

Also on the brighter side, a couple we know retired to one of those talked about vacation climes and has since learned how to politely leave the impression that overnight guests are not necessarily welcome in their paradise. To make the point, they frequently moan about being overwhelmed by all the relatives who come to stay at their home during the cold winters up north. You tend to get the point about dropping in for a visit fairly quickly.

Let us leave this section with some real positives of owning a smaller manse. Done right, you may drastically reduce the maintenance required on a large home – ah the joys of not having to mow a football field or shovel the ski slopes or landscape or clean gutters or weather-proof doorways or – oh you get the point. Note: With each passing year in retirement, the option of not participating in these fun activities becomes more and more attractive.

An Aside: While we just talked a little about the effect of retirement on the children and grandchildren, we are not going to talk a lot about them in future chapters. One reason is that every case with the kids is different. Some will be fine with whatever Mom and Dad do, while others will stress

*over every move. Not only is each case different, but the so-
lutions are also very different from family to family. Rather
than turn our small guide into a very, very large guide, we
would like to leave these solutions to you. After all, you
know so much more about the kids than we will ever be able
to cover.*

4. Sell the family home and rent.

Again, you may rent either in the same city or in a city with a lower
cost of living. Renting has the advantage that you are not putting
down a large amount to buy a new home. *(You do not have to come
up with that 20% down payment if you rent.)* If you plan to rent and –
let us say – you have just sold your house for $250,000, you proba-
bly have to put aside maybe $5,000 to $10,000 for your moving expenses, security deposit, and first month's rent. That leaves at least
$240,000 to go straight into your retirement funds.

Renting has an additional set of advantages over buying. One
advantage of renting is that maintenance, property taxes, and insurance (except for renter's insurance) are now the responsibility of
your landlord. Another is that the fun homeowner activities we
talked about above may now belong to the landlord, such as the lawn
mowing and the shoveling. *(Outside maintenance is also available in
some properties for sale, particularly in condos/condominiums for
seniors, so keep this in mind.)*

**Note: If you buy a new home instead of rent, much of the
profit from the sale of the family home will go into the purchase
of the new house.** If you rent, most of the profit will go into your
retirement savings. Do note that if you rent you will be paying *the
rent* every month for the rest of your retirement, but you will not
have to maintain the property. Here is the place where some realistic
budgeting can be a great help. See Chapter 2.

5. Buy the *retirement* home while still working and living in the *family* home.

This is one option for those with enough money. This option means that you will have to support two homes for what may be a considerable amount of time. When you are ready, you can sell the family home and move into your retirement home. The proceeds from the family home sale become part of the retirement income. However, most of us are not in that kind of financial position.

6. Sell the family home and move to a *cheaper city or town*.

This option can really work well, especially if you trade life in the big city for a smaller, more affordable hometown. (Moving from San Francisco to Santa Fe has been given as an example, although Santa Fe is now getting more expensive.) **This option is probably going to be the savior of a good many of us Boomers and thank heavens. This is especially true if you move to a smaller, less expensive home in the new, less expensive town.**

College towns are often mentioned for their ability to provide a cheaper but nice standard of living. They often have cheap transportation and good, cheap food. You will find college towns listed in a lot of the "Ten places to move for retirement" lists in abundance on the web. If you are careful about where you move, this option is a really strong alternative, as it can save you much more money than you might expect.

When we were younger, we used to joke about what life would be like when all too many of us achieved the golden age of retirement. We envisioned everyone driving at 10 miles per hour, traffic jams at every intersection, waiting forever for the seniors to get through the grocery line, etc. We were sure that most towns would not want "the elderly."

But guess what? Wise communities – as we write this – are actively recruiting seniors. Why? When retirees move to a community, they bring their own money with them (reliable income streams like social security and pensions and dividends) and, through their purchasing, add to the local economy and help produce new jobs. They cost little in services and add through their real estate and construction purchases, retail purchases, and health services.

According to Leading Edge Magazine (Crawford, 2013), the state of Louisiana indicates the economic impact of one new incoming retiree household is equivalent to 3.7 factory jobs. Texas estimates that each retiree household creates 1.5 jobs.

7. Sell the family home and move to a "senior" apartment or home.

The very nice thing about moving to a "senior" apartment house or condo is that everyone there will be about your age. Conversely, the one disadvantage of moving to a "senior" apartment house or condo is that everyone there will be about your age. In addition to some of these apartments built next to a golf course, there are also some amenities that will become very useful, particularly for persons who no longer want to drive or who no longer want to cook all the time. These amenities include transportation to doctors, stores, entertainment, etc. Many also have a restaurant so one does not have to cook every night and lots have a beauty parlor. However, the *rent* and/or *fees* will go up to cover the amenities, often as much as one and a half times to more than two times the rent for a regular apartment or more. This option is expensive.

> *Before dismissing this option, you may want to consider the fact that according to the AARP, 20% of those 65 or over do not drive – that is one in five.*

8. Move into assisted living – Sorry, not yet.

We should mention two housing options you probably are not going to be using at least for a decade or more: assisted living and/or a nursing home. The average age of these two options is around 80 or above. *(We will cover these options in the next book.)*

9. Consider building an ADU – that's Accessory Dwelling Unit.
These ADU's are something new and as of now, are really only available in Portland and a few other cities in the Northwest. These are small units, built normally at the back of a property containing a regular-sized house. (Some are converted garages). In Portland, the maximum allowable size is 800 square feet or 75 percent of the overall square footage of a lot's primary house, whichever is smaller.

What these offer is the ability of the homeowners to rent out the big house (which has more square feet than many retirees need) while the retirees live in the smaller house out back. This allows the family home to be kept in the family, while also providing rent money to pay for expenses for the retirees.

In Portland (Keenan, 2014), the average house is about 668 square feet and costs a little over $80,000. The main problem so far is obtaining loans to build the ADU. This idea seems truly to have much going for it.

Closing Thoughts on the Family Home
The different approaches to using the *family home* listed above are not mutually exclusive. Conditions change as do desires during retirement. The garden next to your home – that you never could get the time to work on while you were working – may be one of your great joys when you first retire. Later, after a few seasons in retirement, that garden may turn into a painful experience (figuratively and literally). Remember, you can change your housing style in retirement.

One last reminder: The "family home" is just another piece of real estate to non-family members. Sometimes even family members develop this view after they have had to help repair the family home. Do include this rather non-sentimental point of view when you examine your options. How many maintenance bills are lurking? What is happening to the neighborhood? Is it stable?

Closing Thoughts on the Family Home and the Kids
One factor which can dramatically affect your choice of housing in retirement is your grandchildren. Many retirees move cross country to retire near their grandchildren. Many others stay in town, again to be closer to their grandchildren.

Both are good choices. The outcomes, however, are not necessarily known ahead of time. A few of them may be disappointing. We bring this up because we have watched some of these outcomes in our friends.

The first is having an expectation of freedom in retirement, only to find that plans are being cancelled because more days than you planned on are being spent in babysitting mode with the grandkids. A second, but different, frustrating outcome is having the expectation of frequent contact with the grandkids, only to find that their parents are doing their best to control contact. Possibly the biggest one of all is finding that the kids themselves do not have the time, or alternatively, do not have the interest. (Compared to soccer or members of the opposite sex, you are definitely lower ranking.)

Before you retire, you may find that a couple of frank conversations may help get everyone's expectations more in line with reality. In retirement, of course, you will find that maintaining a fine sense of balance among everyone's expectations will definitely be called for. One action which may help is to make sure that, wherever you choose to live, you have lots of things to do (not involving the family). You will be happier and your children will not feel as if it is their duty to entertain the grandparents.

More Solutions

Options for More Retirement Income Not Using the Family Home
You may want to look at options for additional retirement income that do not include the family home.

1. Hold off taking social security until full retirement age.

How much you take home depends on the age at which you start taking social security payments. If you enroll at the current full retirement age of 66, you would get 100% of your full benefit each month. But if you started early at 62, you would be entitled to only 75% of your full benefit each month. Conversely, if you can wait to claim benefits until the age of 70, your monthly payout would be 132% of what you would get at age 66. Essentially, each year you can afford to wait increases your benefit, on average over those eight years, by approximately 8% each year.

In addition, Fidelity Investments (Hicken, 2014) estimates that if a couple chooses to retire at the age of 62 instead of 65, they will face $51,000 in additional medical expenses. The major cause is that Medicare coverage does not kick in until age 65. Unless the couple receives coverage from a former employer, they will have to pay for private insurance. With the Affordable Care Act, they cannot be denied insurance. However, they will still face around $17,000 per year in health care premiums and out-of-pocket expenses if they buy insurance on one of the exchanges.

On the get real end, to get the most out of social security means you have to work until you are 70, and I thought we were talking about retirement. However, the later you can wait, the more the payments will be each month. You do not have to wait until 70. Even a couple of years will help. You can check this out at the social security website.

While we are on social security, we need to shout a VERY LARGE WARNING. Let us say that both spouses worked fairly regularly and both have been taking social security. The social security income will be somewhat over $30,000, with let us say around $15,000 apiece. When one member of the pair dies, $15,000 of those payments can disappear. (There is a payment to a beneficiary if that person does not

already receive social security. Widows not already receiv-
ing benefits are due between 71 percent (at age 60) and 100
percent (at full retirement age) of what the husband was
getting before he died. The rules are different, however, if
both husband and wife have been receiving benefits. In this
case, each member of the pair is potentially due two bene-
fits: their own retirement benefit and the benefit on the
spouse's record. However, the surviving member only gets
the one that pays the higher rate, not both.)

If both social security payments are necessary to pay the rent
or mortgage, this means that, on the death of the spouse, a person has
to move. Some may wish to live more simply so having to move is
not a part of the grieving process. (This information is hard to work
with, but we said this would be a "get real" guide and we need to tell
you this.)

2. Get a job.
If you take on a $7.25/hour job and work 32 hours per week, you can
bring in $12,000 a year or $1000 per month. Work for more than the
minimum wage and you will take home even more.

Working 32 hours per week may be okay for some, but it certainly will not pass for retirement for many persons. This may be
your only option. If so, attack the job search with all the expertise
you used in the past.

To insert a little "get real" thinking here, Bankrate (Steiner,
2009), in their Financial Literacy Poll among workers and retirees,
found that 75 percent of non-retirees expect to work for as long as
they can. A total of 39 percent say it's because they like to work.
One-third (32 percent) say it's because they'll need the money. A few
say they'll work for both reasons.

Interestingly, and looking at what happens after one actually
retires, the study found that only 15 percent of today's retirees actually work to supplement their income.

Note: We have reserved our entire last chapter to provide you with lots of great ideas for how to get that job in retirement.

3. Sell your collections.

Ok, who has not grown up listening to Grandma or your Great Aunt explaining the necessity of taking great care of the family silver, grandmother's china, the antique quilts in the cedar chest, and all the rest of the family treasures? Today, we even have better ways of cashing in on the family goodies, starting of course, with eBay and craigslist and other online auctions, as well as a local auction.

And oh, wouldn't it be wonderful if we could turn the family's jewels into real jewels! What is amazing is that sometimes we can do that and other times we cannot. We learned recently that mom's silverware is apt to bring a very nice price – often in almost the same price range as the silverware can be purchased today. Remember to look for silver, not silver plate. On the other hand, our local auctioneer warned us that at auction, the family china would have all the allure of a steaming cup of hot chocolate at a Fourth of July picnic. Moreover, it is worse if that china is not listed as "dishwasher safe" or "microwave safe," what with that beautiful silver/gold rim around the edge. On the other hand, we found at auction that three little silver cream & sugar sets produced a nice return on investment. (Note that these can be melted down for the silver content – sorry about bringing that up).

As an aside, wouldn't it be convenient if we could make good china "hot" again so lots of people would want Grandma's china? Now, if our friends in Seattle could make coffee so very desirable after those days when nobody would drink it, we should be able to put some panache on that family china. (You know, it really is beautiful stuff and it is too bad it is sitting in a box in the basement.)

Some of you may think we are crass in our dealing with the family heirlooms. And we are in a way. Those of you who feel that way may wish to keep the china and silver to "maybe" pass on to your children, and there is certainly a lot right about that approach. However, for those of you with your own china and silver, you may find that a much better use of the family wealth may be to sell some of these items and use the income to build up your retirement savings so that your kids will not have to provide a supplement to you later on.

It is also worth noting that certain types of collectible items can be quite useful. We got near the new purchase price for some Native American jewelry. And, wonder of wonders, we got a lot for two 1950's modern floor lamps in the shape of 2-foot tall eggs. (Honest, they looked great in 1950's décor.)

We do need to include a warning for eBay and other auction novices. Selling successfully at auction requires doing your homework and knowing what you are doing. For each item you are considering putting on an auction site, study the time needed on the auction site to sell the same or similar items, as well as – and this is important – how many just disappear from the site without ever selling. Study how much the items that did sell were bringing in. For example, we were looking at china that sells today for $110 a 5-piece place setting. An identical set – never used and in the original packaging – never sold over a couple of months for more than $50 on eBay, and many identical items did not sell at all. Note that you will have to wrap and send the sold item – so check out shipping before you put the item up. *(If you agree to pay for shipping and you are not careful, you can lose most of what you make with the shipping costs alone.)* You will also pay a commission to the auction. There are also rules for first-time sellers on the auction. Oh yes, as we talked about before, the local auctioneer said not to even bother to put the china up for auction. It would not move. *(That outcome may be better than the three-part sectional couch that did sell for $10. To be honest, that* *couch did not look good in any décor, and that was when it was new.)*

In summary, it is often difficult to determine ahead of time what will sell and what will not among the family treasures. But do include some items that you do not expect to do well – you may be surprised.

There are types of collections that can be considered investments, like stamp or coin collections. Do not forget that you have these and that you may need them later in your retirement.

4. This last item is something you would never expect.

This is also something that may not happen more than once. Our town had a retired teacher who had always lived alone – even into his 80's. All the way through, a next door neighbor had taken it upon herself to watch out for the teacher. As he got older and sicker, the job required more than a little time. But the teacher also asked the neighbor to take on his Power of Attorney and see to things after his death. He also left the house to the neighbor as payment for handling the Power of Attorney, providing the neighbor with the means to finally retire. It is a wonderful story. And it is true. We hope it happens more than once and with an equally good outcome.

What We Did Not Tell You: Medical Expenses

When discussing funds for living in retirement, we have not told you something. You may think that most of your medical costs will be covered by Medicare and a Medicare Part B supplement. However, not everything is covered by these policies, including vision and dental care and the cost of many prescriptions beyond what will be picked up by your Medicare Part D Prescription supplement.

Fidelity (2013) has suggested that today's retirees will need around $220,000 to cover out of pocket medical expenses in retirement. That little sum has *not* been included in the costs needed for retirement above. That is because in the past it was not this much. Our household in retirement has spent over $15,000 in out-of-pocket costs for each of the past two years for medical and insurance expenses, including the premium costs for Medicare, Medicare Part B Supplement and Medicare Part D Prescription Insurance, plus prescription co pays, dental care, and vision care. ***Make sure these medical costs are included in any budgets you make.*** (One recent suggestion is that you want to provide 80% of your pre-retirement income, instead of 70%.)

Note: We do not have a lot of suggestions on how to cut these costs. One is goodrx.com, which compares prices for prescription drugs in *stores in your neighborhood.* The difference from one pharmacy to another can be substantial. Another key thing to remember: the more expensive your prescriptions (what you and the government pay in total), the faster you will go into the doughnut hole. (The doughnut hole may be going away, but it has not disappeared as of mid-year 2014. To be a bit cynical, something like the doughnut hole is likely to be around for a long time, given the "do-nothing" political culture in which we currently live.)

Managing Your Money Once Retired

The next chapter in our Guide should be hints on handling your savings once you have retired. Instead, let us talk a little about what can be expected after you retire.

Oops! This is the first place we went wrong in approaching this topic. Perhaps the single most reliable statement about today's U.S.A. is that we *do not* know what can be expected in the future. At a personal level, we have been amazed by the number of major changes that have taken place since we did our initial retirement planning – long sustained period of low interest rates, high cost of drugs, etc.

The lack of reliable expectations is what is currently driving most of America nuts, and retirees are not different from most Americans. According to our American corporations, they have so far refrained from hiring new workers because there are still too many questions about the future, from health care costs, to expanding regulations, to consumer spending, to an inability of our lawmakers to get along, to how much government is going to spend, etc.

Looking at the late nineties, we are going to point out in the next chapter that Baby Boomers' inability to save for retirement was largely not under Boomers' control. Few of us saw the housing bubble coming or had any influence over it. Few of us saw the tech bubble coming or had any influence over it. A lot of us were caught with health insurance bills large enough to keep a small village in perfect health in more efficient systems and no way around the situation. Too many of us learned how to put out hundreds of resumes without finding a better way.

Our prospects for knowing what is going to happen in the future and for maintaining control over what happens to us are not much better than they were a decade ago. In the 20th century, it was reasonable to expect an 8% return on investments. Now we do not see figures higher than 1-2% in our near future. We see too many proposals from politicians to "save" our Social Security and Medicare by letting us take all the risk.

(If you did not get the drift of that last sentence, "saving" Social Security by getting the government out of social security and by allowing everyone to keep savings in private 401(k)'s means that individuals would risk losing much of their savings every time there is a downturn in the markets. That does not happen with Social Security. Remember that with a 401(k) account, the individual is responsible for investing their contributions to the account, and most is invested in stock market funds. When the stock market tanked in 2008, a lot of money was lost in those accounts. (We are slowly regaining the investments.) Maintaining Social Security and Medicare in a reasonable form for us and for the

*future are two ideas that should turn quiescent Boomers in-
to the activists of all time. Let us hope you are there.)*

Finally, we just do not know when the next "regulation" will
come along to dramatically affect each and every one of us. *(Think of
things like removing the mortgage interest deduction.)*

There is an answer to our dilemma. *(This advice comes from
the one of us who worked over the turn of the century in the financial
sector at one of the nation's largest banks.)* If we do not know where
we are going, the only reasonable way we can handle the future is to
view that future as one of managing *risk*. At each step we need to
look at our situation (and our finances/savings) as one of maintaining
our options so that we do not take excessive risks with our lives and
our portfolios, but that we do take enough risk to take advantage of
situations that are real and positive.

The first rule of managing risk is to understand that managing
risk is not something you do once. Managing risk is an ongoing task.
The second rule of managing risk is to make sure that differing
points of view on possible actions are always there. That means listening to and absorbing lots of information and lots of advice from
lots of perspectives.

Having a certified financial planner is probably a very good
idea for most of us. One caution, however, is to find out how that
planner is being compensated. Some are simply brokers who receive
compensation for buying and selling financial instruments – your
stocks, bonds, mutual funds, etc. – and the more buying and selling,
the more compensation for them. Just be aware with this kind of ana-
lyst that you may have someone more interested in making themselves money than in fostering yours.

A second caution comes concerning advice given last century
by many advisors about how wonderful and stable municipal bonds
are. They are not so stable in the 21st century. These same municipalities we talked about who do not have enough to pay pensions are the

same municipalities who in the future might default on their bonds. In other words, keep current because what is good today may not be good tomorrow.

So we are not going to have a chapter on handling your money after you retire. After all, putting all your attention on building that nest egg should keep you more than busy.

Chapter 5: Why Boomers Are So Pressed for Retirement Savings

In Our Dreams

We have one last topic to cover on money issues. We started off our guide by pointing out two very opposing views of retirement – both of which were in need of a few pinches of reality. The first was the idea that retirement would consist of a series of idyllic happenings certain to keep one endlessly happy. We did warn you that the idyllic scenes were not guaranteed despite those beautiful ads. We did, however, give you many hints to help you avoid NotSoFriendly Town and select a really good retirement mecca.

On the opposite end, we also talked about the dire warnings from too many prognosticators that retirement for Baby Boomers is "going to be an economic catastrophe. Boomers have squandered the savings the generations before them carefully gathered; they have spent money they did not have, etc., etc." So far, we have taken you through more realistic approaches to retirement savings, and we have provided ideas for increasing the retirement funding. What remains is to address why a lot of boomers remain worried about being short on retirement savings.

Get Real Time

A lot of you are still uneasy about your finances. And if you are like us, your blood tends to boil every time you hear someone else blame boomers for "their reckless spending and profligate ways leading us straight into catastrophe."

However, if you take a deeper look into history – especially history in the U.S. since the 1950's – you will understand much more how many of us boomers ended up where we did regarding our retirement savings. **What is most important: you will understand**

that many of us have had no control over happenings which have strongly affected the amount we have been able to save.

Solutions

Mom and Dad in Retirement

Let us go back to how our parents and grandparents retired. Forbes' website (Laura, 2013) recently presented a very comprehensive review of retirement funding over the last century.

Shortly after WWII – in the 1950's – companies desperately needed to attract personnel and did so by offering benefits packages, including retirement plans. These pensions tended to be of the "defined benefit" type. Defined benefit packages offer a specific amount, such as 60% of one's pre-retirement salary, every month for life. Many, if not most, of the defined benefit plans do not require any contribution from the pensioner. The employer is responsible for the entire cost of the pension at retirement (or all but a very small amount).

Importantly, much more than today, one tended to work for the same company until retirement. Many worked tirelessly for the same company until reaching retirement age, received the *gold watch* in a retirement ceremony, and went from there to a well-paid retirement, including that long-planned trip to Europe, allowing us as their friends to be bored beyond measure with the 14-hour slide show of their travels.

As the years passed, however, companies became increasingly aware that people were living longer and costs for these pension programs were getting totally out of control. As such, many companies have been switching to "defined contribution" programs, like a 401(k), where contributions are made by the employee, with little or no matching funds provided by the employer, i.e., the pension cost is now largely or completely borne by the employee.

But wait a minute, these days most of us do not work for the same company throughout our working lives. Large numbers of us have breaks where we were not employed. And because we as the employee were responsible for determining how much we saved, many of us chose (and are choosing) to forego the 401(k) savings (at least for some period of time) in exchange for having money to pay off home equity loans, credit card debt and college loans.

Looking Forward to Us in Retirement

Let us look at examples of some of our cohorts who may not have enough saved for retirement. Below are those who, according to our more judgmental types, *squandered* their money and recklessly lived the good life. *(The names have been disguised, because each example fits a lot of people and one or two may be you or us.)* What becomes so clear below is that **many of these situations were simply not under the control of the person or persons being affected.**

- **Mary and Bill**

  Mary and Bill started their own business in the late 1980's. In the early 1990's, Bill had an angioplasty and Mary had a small tumor removed in outpatient surgery. Very soon after that, their monthly health insurance premium soared to $1800 a month, due to their pre-existing conditions. ($1800 a month in the 1980's translates to over $2800 a month in today's dollars – Ouch.) Because the Portability and Accountability Act did not become effective until the late 1990's, they could not change jobs and keep continuing insurance (via COBRA) until coverage came from the next job. As a result, they hung on until near the turn of the century and watched their business die slowly, due to their costs for insurance making their bids non-competitive. (Health insurance was a real job killer for small businesses in the 1980's and 1990's.)

- **Don**

  As a result of the 1982 recession, Don was laid off his very high paying job as Human Resources Director of a large corporation at the age of 55. He never found another job. While he did receive some early retirement funding, it was nowhere near the full retirement he would have received had he be able to work until 65. (The early 80's is the first time we really became aware that companies were laying off high level professionals as a simple matter of course when company revenues were less than expected.)

• June and Jeff

June and Jeff were both highly paid IT professionals until 2002, when both were laid off (from different companies) less than a month before Christmas as part of the Tech Bubble bursting. *(Talk about the Christmas Grinch.)* It was early 2004 before the household had income again. *(All along, the two had counted on their two incomes to keep them in the upper middle income range, but after 2004 only one income was coming in for much of the time and that includes the fact that their IT skills were up-to-date and high level. So much for that shortage of all types of STEM workers.)*

• James

In 2008, James at the ripe old age of 58 was laid off in the Great Recession and is still job hunting today. Enough said.

• Martin's Parents

Martin, age 28, received his MBA a year ago from one of the nation's more prestigious universities and is still living at home, looking for a job appropriate for his education and debt load and using up some of the income that Martin's parents should be putting away for retirement, not to mention Martin's incredibly high college costs which previously affected his parents' retirement funds.

• Joan

Joan, a medical billing coder, has been on unemployment for over a year, but she cannot accept a lower paying job because her mortgage requires a higher salary. Take just any job, and she loses her home of 20 years. *(She did not buy a home she could not afford and she should not be expected to lose that house because she takes "just any job," instead of one that pays what her skills should command.)*

• Dan

After watching housing prices skyrocket from 2004-2005, Dan, age 44, took out a home equity loan to renovate his kitchen to make his house easier to sell. Now, housing prices are picking up after the Great Recession (but not all the way), so he will still lose $20,000-30,000 after he pays off the mortgage and home equity loan. *(Important: he really cannot change jobs for a better one until he sells the home. As of April, 2014, 17% of all U.S. residential properties with a mortgage were still seriously under water.)*

• George and Marion

Up until 2014, George and Marion were paying $2000 per month for their high risk pool health insurance. Both were refused health insurance by numerous insurance companies due to pre-existing medical conditions. George takes a statin for high cholesterol and Marion uses Metrogel, an anti-acne cream – both reasons to deny insurance in one or more states until Obamacare. *(Please note that George and Marion were frequently referred to as the "very sick" people we cannot afford to allow to get insurance. Also note that pre-existing conditions were a problem for Mary and Bill and their business in the early '90s but it took until 2014 to get the problem addressed.)*

Looking at the cases above, there was very little that those being harmed could do to improve their situation. They were caught and had to make the best of it.

We also should note that many in the list above tended to use credit cards and home equity loans to carry them through their financial crises, which in the long run reduced their savings for retirement. For the most part, what happened to the folks above – i.e., overused credit lines – did not happen to their parents and grandparents, if only because credit was not so readily available in those times.

The Great Divide: Is It Coming?

Now let us look at some other folks – Boomers whose luck has been a bit better. Mark works for the State government where they live and Janine is a teacher. Neither has had to worry about layoffs because they both have tenure. Since they have held these jobs since shortly after graduation from college, they will be eligible for retirement at age 55. (The "rule of 85," used by many government entities, allows one to retire when the years worked plus the age equals 85 or greater.) Like many government jobs, Mark and Janine will be paid 60 % of their last salaries for life and will also likely receive health insurance paid until they reach 65, as well as social security. Mark and Janine will take home over $100,000 per year when they do retire.

You may be starting to see "The Great Divide" among retirement couples. Too many baby boom retirees are going to retire with substantially less funding than originally counted upon. On the other side will be many public sector employees and some private sector employees who will still be able to take advantage of the defined benefit pension. In fact, we do know that friends of ours who have already retired with government pensions have been *admonished* by their friends that they are taking home far more than most in their social group and they might want to downplay their good fortune. (If you are one of the better off ones, keep reading. We have tips for all retirees.)

Now, in all fairness, we do not know yet whether all the employers who still have defined benefit plans will come through with the full retirement promised to many of those public sector employees. *(As we write this section, the world is waiting to see how Detroit in bankruptcy will handle its pension obligations. Initially retirees were being asked to give up 27% of their retirement funds. The percent then moved down to 4.5%, and retired workers did accept the reduction. However, the ultimate success of the plan depends on consistent and strong investment returns for the city, in a period of low interest rates and significant volatility. The bankruptcy judge, Steven W. Rhodes, has noted that his greatest concern arises from the risks that the city retains relating to its pension funding (Walsh, 2014). Detroit's retirees face an uncertain and likely uncomfortable future.)*

Summing up

OK, let us review. Few of us are going to have all the money we would like to have to retire. But, for most of us in the 401(k) generation, it is not because we did something wrong. It is not because we overspent or because we squandered our money away or because we did not try.

We have also talked about how many of our parents came out so far ahead of us. The trick was in employee retirement plans, and specifically, defined benefit plans to which our parents did not have to make large contributions. Steady employment played a very large role, also. Not everyone had a pension, but most had steady employment. As such, they could save to supplement their social security, and look forward to Tuesdays in Belgium.

In contrast, a study out of the RAND group (Browning, 2011) found that since the Great Recession, about 39% of all Americans have been foreclosed upon, unemployed, underwater, or behind 2+ months on their mortgage. Think of it this way – those really bad things happened to four of your neighbors (or three of your neighbors and yourself), out of the ten households on your block.

And finally, it is not difficult to see that when there are two or more unemployed persons for every available job, one does not *choose* to work rather than taking unemployment benefits, as some of our better-off cohorts seem to think.

Retirement Now a Personal Responsibility

> *Forbes magazine (Laura, 2013) notes that given everything that has happened, it is surprising that Baby Boomers are not further behind.*

> *Unlike the situation for past generation retirees, retirement for boomers is now a personal responsibility, i.e., many, many boomers are going to have to fund up to 70% of their own retirement.*

Planning for the Future

In the spirit of *get real* thinking, one has to wonder at the large difference in retirement income between those with a defined benefit plan and those without and whether this will cause problems between the two groups in the future. The defined benefit plans still alive today tend to be offered by government entities at all three levels – local, state, and federal government – although many of these are now being replaced by a variety of defined contribution plans. They also tend to provide full benefits because *tenure* is also a part of many government jobs. Once tenure is achieved, it is very difficult to lay someone off, thus producing employees with unbroken employment records. And while this all sounds wonderful, too many municipalities are discovering that their pension funds are way underfunded. The extent to which these plans may or may not pay out for future retirees is still unknown, partly because they depend on future economic growth and associated tax revenue. We will have to wait and see.

Chapter 6: Living Independently or Living with Others

In Our Dreams

The one thing we can be assured about Baby Boomers (i.e., us) is that most of us will fight like crazy to live independently as long as we can. You may also have noticed that, presently, we are also ready to attack any signs of "growing old" with the vehemence of Godzilla on steroids. This includes – horror of horrors – those pesky little brown spots on our skin. *(It is amazing that we now have a thousand new products on the market to erase the little brown spots. It is even more amazing that none of those we have tried seem to work very well. Sorry. Did you think this book was going to solve all your problems?)* And finally, do we really have to bring up that "65 is the new 45"?

Get Real Time

Normally, our "Get Real Time" section points out the divergence of our dreams from reality. However, this case is different. While wanting to remain independent as long as possible is admirable, it is also eminently practical. As past generations got old, there was normally a daughter or other family member to take care of the folks. These days, daughters and other family members are working and these families often cannot put their own lives on hold while they lose a family member to elder caregiver. This is not going to get better in the near future. (Often the need to provide a family caregiver comes as a family is trying to get back on their feet after one of today's disasters, such as a job loss or health problem. It certainly happened to us.)

Solutions

But never fear. Each day, more and more services open up to take care of us. There are four tricks to successfully living independently.

• **Stocking up on important items needed to live independently.**

• **Identifying important needs.**

• **Hunting down services/getting specific information about those services**

• **Making sure that the sources are safe: checking with the Better Business Bureau.**

(We are not going to talk a lot about checking businesses out before you buy, but we cannot stress how important it is to make sure you are not going to be overcharged, under serviced, bullied, and/or relieved of your worldly goods.)

1. Stocking Up on Important Items – If You Can Pick It Up, You Will Drop It

Starting at the beginning, you really know the Old Age Gremlin is upon you when you realize that if you pick it up you probably will drop it. This old age problem probably comes about because, as we age, we become less flexible and therefore we do not always move to where we want to put object X down. Short of goal, object X ends up on the floor and getting to the floor to pick up object X is a real pain at our "advanced age." Worse yet, as time marches on, there will be days when it seems like all we do is pick up what we have dropped.

There is one simple solution. We call it the "picker upper" – a long-handled grab tool which is so useful in picking up what you have dropped that we have one in the living room, the dining room, the bedroom, and the bath, and we frequently need one in between. (They often give these away free upon the purchase of an electric scooter, or they cost under $20 on Amazon or at the drugstore.)

Having a picker-upper is the first step in living independently. All children should make sure that the folks are prepared in this
important area. (While we are here, we should also mention that extremely useful is an item to help put on socks, as well as various
items which will help you open jars.)

2. Identifying Important Needs

This chapter on living independently is particularly difficult to write,
because most of you in your 60's are going to feel pretty good. Your
needs will be few, and you will be anxious to get out in the world
and move. However, at some point in your 60's (we are guessing)
you may begin to notice that it might be simply more convenient or
pleasant to have help or have somebody else do it. Our big surprise
was that, as we added a few years, the hard part in life was going
down the stairs, not going up. We never would have guessed.

Many areas of need will come along much more slowly and
many more will never arrive. (My mom was touring Russian palaces
in her 80's.) On the other hand, while we joke about getting Uncle
Ed to stop driving in his 90's, about one in five (according to the
AARP) of those 65 and older no longer drive. This means that transportation to doctors, pharmacies, grocery stores, big boxes, hair cutters, banks and club meetings may become an issue, as well as services to deliver groceries and prescriptions and the evening meal.
And even if one of you still drives or a family member has offered, it
is still useful to be able to get around totally on your own. Thanks to
the Americans with Disabilities Act (ADA), cities are now better
prepared than ever to get you from A to B and most important, easily
and affordably with or without the aid of a walker, cane, or other
mobility device.

(Speaking personally, the inability of one of us to drive has
been devastating really to both of us. It strips us of the free-
dom to move, it leads to personal dependency, and it pro-
duces an unbalanced workload for us as a couple. It is more

*serious than any of us admit, and it really is depressing.
And it is why the ADA transportation directives are so important.)*

As for most other needs, we are guessing that later on the desire to never clean your house again will arise, and later than that, the
desire to welcome those lovely folks from Meals on Wheels. Finally,
your kids through all of this will be panicked over your safety – in
some cases rightfully so and in others, not so much.

**Below is a list of services we all might need at one time or an-
other:**

• **Transportation/ Getting Around/ Buses and Taxis.**
Here there is a wide range of options from a little to lots of
help to live independently. We will cover more on this later.

• **Food Shopping/Delivery.**
This task comes up once or twice a week, at a minimum.
There is little way around it. Fortunately, some food stores
are now offering delivery.

• **Big Box Shopping.**
This type of shopping is perhaps not as frequent as food
shopping, but these stores seem to go from lots of selection –
to big – to cavernous – to inconvenient for many of us.

• **Meals On Wheels/Meal Delivery.**
You may be in your 90's when you need this, but when you
do, it will be key to health and wellbeing.

• **Medications Obtained/Delivery.**
You may think now that this is just an ordinary part of life –
no big deal. However, if you have not faced the Medicare
rules on how frequently and when you can refill a prescription and your doctor has not been keeping up in prescribing
lots of pills to keep you going, you have no idea what is in

store. For some, like a person taking the new meds following a heart attack, some prescription or another comes up for a refill every other day, and you cannot find any way to make the days between refills come out so you can refill more than one at a time. We have had to get refills so frequently that we have suggested that our pharmacy offer overnight stays. This problem for many of us may well rank as *Frustration #1 for living independently*.

- **Health Care Management/Trips To Doctors.**

    A common complaint we hear among the already retired is that trips to doctors are overtaking their life – that is in between getting the prescriptions filled. Please note that the greater the number of meds prescribed, the more frequently one has to be checked out by one's doctor. Judging by comments from others and our own experience, this problem can easily rank for many of us as *Frustration #2 for living independently*.

- **Medications/Help In Taking On Schedule.**

    This item seems simple on the surface. However, as an example, too many of us are going to be diagnosed as having Type 2 Diabetes. The schedules for taking the diabetic medications are quite complicated and yet it is vital that they are followed religiously.

- **Personal care/Hair cutters.**

    Ah! Finally something we might enjoy. In addition, as we age, pedicures will become not only fun, but necessary, because you see, the older you get, the bigger the distance between you and your feet – believe us.

- **Home Maintenance/Management.**

    This task tends to be overlooked, yet having a clean house once every couple of weeks can do wonders, not only for the temperament, but also for your safety. There is one humongous warning here. It is seldom recognized, but one of the most dangerous jobs in home maintenance is getting down on all fours to drain a sprinkler system in the fall, especially for the over 60 crowd. Here is one place we all should use help and there are many others. Fortunately, most services in this area can be bought on the open market without having to find a "senior" service.

- **Financial Maintenance/Management.**
  As we get older and spacier, having a little help organizing and paying bills, as well as managing one's retirement savings may become very necessary, and most necessary here is having help from someone you can really trust.

- **Products & Services To Make Life Better.**
  - Help getting to activities/the Senior Center/Newcomer's Club,
  - In-home care – a wide range of help in the home for $19-$25 an hour.
  Includes activities like those listed below for the nationwide firms, plus help in miscellaneous areas like "help me hang a picture."
  - Learning to keep up: The digital world/MOOC's/ and all things new.
  - Life Alert, Jitterbug phone, Twitter, Facebook, cell phone.
  Includes all things geared to keeping you involved and safe.

- **Getting Information.**
  The last item above brings up an item of necessity. Getting help requires getting information and these days, getting information requires *becoming facile* using search functions on a computer, iPad, laptop, or smart phone. If you do not have this in your repertoire, now is the time to get it. The easiest

way to do this is to contact your local library. Almost all have mini programs to teach basic computer skills.

3. Hunting Down Specific Senior Care Services

Putting "services for seniors" in a search engine will show you both the large number and the range of services dedicated to senior care offered by the federal, state, and local governments, by non-profit organizations, and by profit-making corporations. While this is a good start, what we found from this type of top-level search is that most were simply telling us that they offered "services for seniors," along with a mission statement, i.e., "assist older adults in maintaining health, dignity, quality of life, and independence by delivering services and programs." Most also did provide a phone number to call. Unfortunately, what we really wanted was to find out how to get a ride to the doctor's office next Tuesday at 10 a.m.

Before turning to getting the specific services, it is helpful to list three useful items which do tend to show up on the more general sites. These are frequently good places to start.

- **A list of national or state (often franchised) organizations for senior services.**

  Three examples of the many available are: *A Place for Mom* (a free service providing reviews of housing options), *Home Instead* (help in staying at home), and something like *Seniors Helping Seniors* (a service using seniors to help seniors).

- **A list of senior service organizations accredited by the BBB.**
  (If this does not come up, look up the Better Business Bureau specifically.)

- **A list of your city's Senior Service Center/other government organizations.**

4. Getting What You Really Need

For specific information on a topic, we found the best route to be searching the topic directly, such as "transportation for seniors," or "buses for the disabled," or "taxis for seniors," followed by the name of your city. Often this will get you to the Department of Transportation for the state or locality. Information is provided on how to obtain the transport, cost, time needed to reserve, to cancel, etc. Fortunately for all, the ADA (Americans with Disabilities Act) requires that "all fixed route, public transit buses be accessible and that supplementary para-transit services be provided for those individuals with disabilities who cannot use the fixed route bus service." Also, be sure to contact local hospitals & health organizations who often provide transport for doctors' appointments.

In summary, the more specific the Google search (i.e., "Safeway delivery"), the better chance you have of finding what you really need.

5. How the Family Can Help

One way the family might be able to help without interfering in your life would be to prepare a "Senior Services Guide" for you and the family, based on your specific needs. Making a guide is not going to be the simplest task in the world. It basically will involve lots of hours using search functions and a couple of hours on the phone. However, for those of you worried that your grandkids are computer savvy (i.e., excellent at games, Twitter, Instagram, Pinterest, Facebook, etc.) but not necessarily computer knowledgeable, how better to move forward than to see if the kids/grandkids would like to help grandma and grandpa by making a Senior Services Guide specifically for them. (Or even simpler, on the grandparent's laptop/computer, tablet or smartphone, they could "bookmark" or put on the "favorites" list hyperlinks to useful sites with senior services.)

The one trick kids need to know to optimize their internet searches is to search using the exact terms apt to be found in the articles they need. This is an iterative task. At each step, the kids should look carefully at the titles for the pages they find useful and start using those words in the next search. Then repeat for the next round, using the pages found useful in the last search as the words selected for the next search.

If the task of producing a Senior Citizens Guide could be made part of a school or club project for the kids, guides can be given to grandparents of club members and the rest can be passed out at senior service organizations.

Below are some examples of the information useful in a Senior Services Guide. For each example, we arbitrarily selected a city and looked at one option for providing that service. This is just to give you an idea of the type of information out there. And more important, it will tell you what you might expect in your own hometown and what you might be asked to provide or to do in order to use the service. CAUTION: Do not accept the information here. Instead, do look up your local area and because things change, do not accept what is here even if it sounds like your city. Look up everything anew.

Services to Meet Specific Needs

National/Franchised Services

• Seniors Helping Seniors

Seniors Helping Seniors offers non-medical aid in the following areas: cooking, light housekeeping, companionship, personal grooming and dressing, shopping, doctor visits, transportation, yard work, mobility assistance, house maintenance and small repairs, overnight stays (24-hour care), long-distance check-ins, respite care, Alzheimer/Dementia care. All of the helpers are seniors themselves. Services are provided in the home for older adults who want to stay in their homes at reasonable hourly rates. "We can reduce your worry by checking in on your parents if you live too far and by helping out with a weekly 2 – 3 hour check-in and getting some chores done like checking the fridge, shopping, preparing nutritious meals, cleaning out the bathroom and checking on medications."

- **A Place for Mom (You may want this for your parents – i.e., those guys in their 90's.)**

  A Place for Mom is a free resource helping families find assisted living facilities, dementia care, Alzheimer's memory care, and nursing home care. They provide advisors to help an aging parent make the transition from living independently or with family to accepting outside assistance or moving to a senior living community. They provide help in assessing needs, in getting information on facilities that best meet needs, and assistance in visiting communities at the senior's own pace.

- **Home Instead**

  Home Instead Senior Care provides help with senior home care services delivered right in the home. They can provide care either a few hours a day or long-term care 24 hours a day. All caregivers are thoroughly screened, extensively trained, insured and bonded, matched to your preferences, professional and reliable. Some interesting services they list include: check food expirations, assist with entertaining, care for houseplants, oversee home deliveries, mail bills and letters, assist with laundry and ironing, take out garbage, provide medication reminders, organize mail, change linens, assist with pet care, accompany to appointments, escort for shopping and errands.

Examples of Specific Services

Senior Transportation Example

Dial-A-Ride in a Moderately-sized Mountain West town.

(To repeat, you will want to do one specifically for your town.) Dial-A-Ride provides Door to door paratransit service for individuals who, because of a disability, are prevented from using the city's fixed route bus service. All trips must remain within the revised service area, which is defined as ¾ mile from any fixed bus route. Dial-A-Ride operates from 6:00 AM - 11:00 PM Monday through Saturday, except for published holidays. Fares are $2.50 per one-way trip. Trip Reservations must be made at least one day in advance. Reservations are taken up to 14 days in advance.

The first time you call, they will get your name and address in order to send you information and eligibility forms. This process will take up to 21 calendar days to process upon receipt of the application. Please note that an application is not considered complete until a health care provider verification form has been received.

To help ensure Dial-A-Ride will get you to your destination on time be ready at least 15 minutes before your pickup time, be prepared to wait up to 15 minutes after your pickup time, and watch for your driver.

Grocery Delivery Example

Grocery Chain in a Moderately-sized Southwestern Town
This store delivers 7 days a week between 10:00 am and 10:00 p.m. They provide 1-Hour delivery windows, enabling one to schedule a grocery delivery at an available time that perfectly fits a tight schedule. It is also possible to save money by selecting an available 2-Hour window or an environmentally friendly "Green" 4-Hour window.

A $49 minimum purchase amount (excluding applicable tax, delivery fee, fuel surcharge, bottle deposits and bag fees where applicable) is required to process and deliver your order. Regular home delivery rates in most areas are $9.95 on purchases of $150 or more (excluding applicable tax, delivery fee, fuel surcharge, bottle deposits and bag fees where applicable) and $12.95 on purchases under $150 (excluding applicable tax, delivery fee, fuel surcharge, bottle deposits and bag fees where applicable). A fuel surcharge may apply.

"Shop By History" is the *fastest* way to shop. Items purchased with a registered Club Card, both in-store and online, are saved in a personal "Shop By History." A cart can be filled in minutes, since all recent purchases are already on 1 page. No need to create a separate shopping list. The order is selected the day of delivery and loaded onto the store's delivery trucks. Trucks are equipped with multiple temperature zones, so frozen items stay frozen and vegetables are crispy fresh when delivered.

Someone over the age of 18 must be present to accept delivery of the online order. To ensure quality, deliveries are not left unattended. Visa, MasterCard, Discover and American Express credit cards, and debit cards that have a Visa or MasterCard logo are accepted. Cash, gift cards, Fast Forward, personal checks and other charge accounts are currently not accepted online.

Meals on Wheels Example

Meals on Wheels in a Medium-sized Southwestern Town.
"Meals on Wheels" is in most cities in the U.S. Individual cities will vary in the specific services provided (such as the ability to meet special dietary needs), as well as in the price of the meals. We have listed below the services offered in one city in the U.S. to give you an idea of what might be involved. Be sure to check your own city for exact details.

"Meals on Wheels" in this city delivers 140,000 meals a year to the homes of those unable to prepare meals in their own homes. In addition the food delivery also provides a friendly smile to the recipient and the knowledge that someone each day is checking on recipients to make sure they are safe and healthy and not in medical distress.

A regular meal consists of a hot entrée, 2 vegetables, milk or juice, bread, salad, and either fruit or a dessert. A registered dietician works with the program to ensure that special diets are served. Meals are delivered by volunteers between 10:30 a.m. and 1:30 p.m. Monday through Friday. Someone must be home to accept the meal as meals cannot be left un-refrigerated.

Full pay clients pay $6.30 per hot meal in our example city – payable by check or credit card. (Many cities charge less.) Financial assistance may be available if meal costs represent a hardship. The recipient, a family member, or a professional caregiver may apply by telephone. The application process takes approximately 15 minutes.

Pharmacy Delivery Example

Chain Pharmacy in a Large Southern Town.
This store offers Same Day Delivery Service using FedEx Same Day City Service. Delivery is available within 5 miles of a store in the area. A list of participating stores is provided. The first step is to enroll in Express Pay using a credit card on the store's secure server.

Same day delivery is only offered for prescriptions ordered in stores. Delivery cannot be placed online for this same day delivery service. (The pharmacy also offers full service for online ordering and delivery, which takes a few days.) To make the order, either call or visit the pharmacy. A two prescription minimum is needed for the Same Day service. An adult signature is required at delivery. Delivery will be by FedEx Same Day City Service. A $5 delivery fee may be charged.

Life Alert Example

Online Ordering.
Life Alert® is a medical alert system specifically designed to protect seniors and all family members in a home health emergency. Life Alert® services can help seniors remain independent and possibly avoid a retirement home by sending help fast in the event of fall, fire, CO Gas, poison, and home invasion emergencies.

Getting help is as simple as the push of a button even if you cannot reach a phone, allowing independent seniors to live alone without ever being alone.

Jitterbug Phone Example

Online Ordering.

Jitterbug® is an easy-to-use cell phone and medical alert device in one. The phone is senior friendly with big buttons, large numbers, a loud clear speaker, and "Yes" and "No" navigation keys. In addition, Jitterbug® provides a network of health & safety experts. In uncertain or unsafe situations, you can speak immediately with an NAED certified Response Agent, who can confirm your location, evaluate your situation, and get you the help you need.

You can also speak with a live nurse or doctor, as well as get daily reminders to help you stay on your prescription schedule.

At the time of writing, data plans start from just $2.49 per month, offering the most affordable plans on the market.

Chapter 7: Move or Age in Place

In Our Dreams

Retirement for me always included images of the two of us hiking in our beloved Rocky Mountains. That is when we were a lot younger and the whole world of retirement was before us. And then in my late 50's, I slipped in the tub.

Get Real Time

What I did to myself just does not happen, but it did to me. *(They have not called me klutz for 50 years for nothing.)* On the way down, my left shin slammed into the tub with the speed and force of a karate chop – Ah Cha!!

We should have guessed something was really wrong when the shin remained seriously numb *(did not hurt at all)* for three weeks. It was at the end of the 3 weeks that I discovered that every step I was going to take from then on was going to be memorable, and that additional problems related to the injury would develop later on.

I bother to tell you this because – way, way too early, I learned what getting to be in my late 80's or 90's is going to be like. Well, I am not usually as grouchy as those other folks, but I can now go up and down 1-2 steps at most and I can walk less than 30 feet before I need to sit. Way too early, I know what "elderly" means.

Solutions

In early retirement many of you are going to be putting down significant amounts of cash for a new place to live – either buying or renting and either in your home town or away. Now, what happened to me is not going to happen to you, but now, when you probably have a little more cash than you will have later, is a good time to think ahead and do the prep for those days when you might be a little less mobile.

Why do we suggest this? Well, we just moved from our previous home because:

- **The walker did not fit through the bathroom door.**
  Note that homes built in the 1960's tend to have very narrow doorways and very narrow halls.

- **The laundry was in the lower level.**
  Getting there involved going down a flight of very narrow steps – no longer accessible to me.

- **There was no way in or out of the house (3 entrances) that did not involve at least three steps.**
  None had a stable railing right at the entrance and none was amenable to a ramp.
  Net, net, now is a good time to examine your current family home, as well as any places you are considering renting or buying.

Getting More Comfortable Now

Below are a number of steps that – although these are not things to be done strictly for a disability or mobility problem – are things to consider simply because it is more comfortable that way.

- **Consider replacing that older toilet.**
  Putting in a new 17" to 19" high comfort toilet is one thing you will really appreciate and that is not really expensive. New toilets can cost as little as $100 if you do the installation.

- **Install grab bars by the tub and toilet.**
  Alternatively, check that the bath walls are reinforced to be appropriate for the later installation of the grab bars. (The bars go such a long way to let you make sure that when the

time comes to have your knees/hips replaced, it will be voluntary.)

• **Look for chairs with arms well forward and high.**
This will make it so much easier to get up, even for a nimble 50-year-old.

• **Make sure all throw rugs are well anchored or get rid of them.**
(You do know that your grandchild will also recommend this step as part of her home safety audit for school.)

• **Put a shower chair or spa stool (beautiful in teak) in your shower or tub.**

• **Consider a hand held shower head with a long (6-foot) hose.**
(You may as well be comfy in that shower, as well as in a soaking bath.)

• **Consider door levers instead of knobs.**
It is easier on the hands.

Getting More Comfortable in the Future
Before going further, we need to introduce three terms – needed for your Google/Internet searches.

1. Accessible Design
The Fair Housing Act of 1988 (covers private multi-family dwellings) and the Americans with Disabilities Act of 1990 (covers commercial and public facilities) lay out requirements for ensuring that these dwellings and facilities are accessible by those with physical disabilities.

2. Aging in Place
Aging in Place conveys the idea that the elderly would prefer to age while remaining in their home (as opposed to an assisted living facility or nursing home). The CDC defines Aging in Place as "the ability

to live in one's own home and community safely, independently, and comfortably."

3. Universal Design

The National Association of Home Builders (NAHB) refers to universal design as the design of products and environments to be usable by all people, to the greatest extent possible, without the need for adaptation or specialized design. A Certified Aging in Place Specialist (CAPS) can help remodel your home using universal design concepts.

Design features recommended by NAHB include such items as:

• Main living occurring on a single story, including a full bath.

• 5 x 5 foot clear turning space (for a wheelchair/scooter/ walker/etc.)

This should be provided in the living room, kitchen, a bedroom, and a bath.

• A surface to put packages on when opening a door.

• Wall support/provision for later on being able to adjust the height of kitchen counters and cabinets.

This involves moving counters and upper cabinets down so someone in a wheelchair can reach and the ability to remove a lower cabinet for a wheelchair to move into the space. This item simply requires a little thought during the initial design and build of the space – it may never have to be used, but simply specifies such things as a removable drawer at the bottom of a lower cabinet so you could later remove the drawer and move the cabinet down if necessary. Big deal.

• **Base cabinets with roll out trays and lazy susans.**

• **Washer and dryer 12-15 inches above the floor (if both front-loading).**

This makes it easier if you are in a wheelchair.

• **Home wired for security. Home wired for computers.**

• **Fold down seat in the shower.**

• **Adjustable hand-held shower head with a long 6-foot hose.**

If you want to see these items carried out beautifully, look up the Aging Beautifully website on the net – agingbeautifully.org. The place is magnificent and few would ever guess it is set up for all kinds of physical disabilities. Wonderfully, most of the accommodations are fairly inexpensive, but do require thought during the initial design/build.

Most people are not going to go to these ends, but it is great to know there is lots of help if needed.

What to Look For in a New Apartment
The Fair Housing Act requires that all multi-unit dwellings with 4 units or more and without an elevator should have all ground floor units accessible. *(If there is an elevator, all units in a 4+ dwelling should be accessible.)* These requirements should be in place for dwellings built after 1991, but there is no enforcement beyond filing lawsuits, so you do need to look. We found few accessible dwellings in NotSoFriendly Town.

We are in an accessible apartment and love every minute of it. You do not have to encounter slippery stairs when the weather is bad. And inside you feel so much less cramped – like you are living in a much larger space.

Items you are apt to see include:

• **No stairs/accessible through at least one entrance into the unit.**

• **No stairs/accessible throughout the public use areas of the complex.**

• **No stairs/accessible throughout the main living areas of the unit.**

• **Grab bars in the bath or walls reinforced to accommodate grab bars to be put in later.**

• **Five-foot turnaround in the bath.**

• **Hallways 36 inches wide (recommend 42 inches or more).**

• **Doorways with at least 32-inch pass through.**

• **Levers on doors, no doorknobs.**

• **Electric 15 inches or more off the floor.**

• **Light switches no higher than 48 inches off the floor.**

• **Laundry accessible.**

About "The Ramp" and Other Signs the Elderly Live Here

The nicest thing about the accessible apartment where we live is that it does not scream, "Elderly and disabled live here". I doubt you would have any idea unless we told you. In fact, I know you would not.

Further, when you plan ahead, ADA compliant construction either costs about the same or tends to accrue upcharges in the realm of 5%. For example, concrete stairs actually cost more than putting in ramping (i.e., sloping the concrete up an incline) and the ramping can look as if it is part of the landscaping.

You have no idea how much you will appreciate that ramp 1) when junior breaks his leg on a skateboard, 2) when you have your knee replacements, 3) when 90-year-old Aunt Flo comes to visit, and 4) when putting in the ramp allows you to decrease the lawn area to be watered and mowed.

One of the nicest ramps we know is camouflaged behind raised flower planters. The planters go across the front yard and then back again to the front door, slowly sloping upward at they go. Berms with flower beds or, better yet, year-round conifer or other evergreen plantings are other routes.

Finally, remember that we old folk are going to be increasing in large numbers in the near future as we Baby Boomers retire. Making some of these changes should definitely go toward increasing a home's value for selling, particularly if these are done discreetly and with taste – no screaming please.

Realistic Changes You Might Really Want to Make
So, in one step you can plan for *really old* age and increase the value of your home, making it easier to sell, should you decide not to age in place. Below are some realistic changes you might seriously consider:

- **Moving the laundry upstairs.**

- **Getting one full bath on the main living floor.**

- **Levers on the doors instead of knobs.**

- **Side by side fridge.**
  A side by side makes both freezer and refrigerator accessible to a wheelchair user.

- **Identify areas in home where a one or two step transition could be replaced with a platform lift.**

- **Level entrance into the shower.**

- **Seat in shower.**

Chapter 8: Staying Healthy

In Our Dreams

One of the great things about retirement is being able to get out and do all those things you never had time to do. As they say, "retirement is when we pay ourselves to do the things we love." You can take your pick: biking around town, hiking up a mountain trail, swimming in sky blue tropical waters, antiquing in a small new England town, playing computer games with the grandkids, running with your four-footed friends, etc., etc., etc.

In fact, the newest research (Fell, 2012) has recently come out saying it is OK to keep up your running routine as you get older. Continuing to run does <u>not</u> seem to produce the often expected bad effects according to two groups of Stanford researchers. The first group studied long-distance runners older than 50 and reported that their bone mineral content *(protects against fractures)* was 40% higher, on average, than in control subjects. The second group of re-searchers at Stanford found no difference in the risk of osteoarthritis in the knees of runners compared to the control. All right, already! Way to go!

Get Real Time

Oh yes, there is one little thing we forgot to tell you. The latest pre-diction for retirees (Fidelity, 2013) is that a couple retiring today at 65 will need around $220,000 just to cover medical expenses (in-cludes Medicare Part A & B premiums, Medicare Part B Supplement Premiums, Medicare Part D Prescription Premiums, vision and den-tal care, and the out-of-pocket costs for prescriptions that are not covered by Part D). Importantly, these expenditures are beyond what is traditionally included in the usual retirement funds.

I can hear you say, "Why is no one telling me this? Why is it not in most of the material I have been reading?" Well, it never used to be this bad. We know it is real, though, because we have seen it with our own eyes. Last year we had over $15,000 in out-of-pocket medical costs (that is, those listed in the previous paragraph and not covered except by our checkbook). Much of this was simply for medications not covered by Medicare or any insurance.

All right, you say, but this will not happen to me. I have taken very good care of myself. I eat right. I exercise. I am in good shape physically. This clearly will not happen to me. It may not. I have known three persons who in their late 80's and 90's were in great health, saw doctors only occasionally, and took very few meds.

Now about the rest of us: As we get older, we will regularly see our main physician. At some point, one or more of our blood measures will be off, and the doc will prescribe something to help for one of these chronic (meaning it goes on and on) problems. Fortunately, with recent advances in modern medicine, even those with very serious medical problems (heart, lungs, etc.) can lead very productive and very long lives with these newer medications. However, let me tell you: The medications are expensive and a surprising number are not covered by insurance. Further, there is no relief in sight because none of us wants to give up the possibility of leading that longer, productive life.

There is also the problem of deteriorating parts: knees, hips, shoulders. Half of our close friends have already replaced a part or two. My crystal ball foresees even more in the future.

One critical need is for Baby Boomers to make sure they are there to stand up on the side of needed Medicare and Social Security benefits. We simply cannot afford to lose these benefits to benign neglect and/or well-meaning conservatives who have not yet faced these costs. In the meantime, below are some other steps to help you thread your way successfully through 21st century medical care.

Solutions

1. First and foremost in our list is: Keep those medical receipts.
Do keep all of them – including travel costs to doctors and pharmacies. Make sure you take a look at deducting those expenses on your taxes. For medical tests, they belong to you and you should be able to ask for a copy of any medical test and it should be provided.

2. Compare prices.
Prices tend to change. We discovered recently that a pharmacy we had been using for some high priced prescriptions *(because three years ago they were low cost)* was now very pricey for those same prescriptions. There are websites that provide comparisons of *local* prices for a wide variety of prescriptions. One notable one is goodrx.com.

Even if you do not think that you care about the "standard" price because the copay (what you pay) remains the same, a higher price will land you in the *donut hole* quicker. *(The total price – what you pay plus what Medicare pays – is what is added to get to the entry into the donut hole.)* That means that your prescriptions for the rest of the year will be more expensive. (Oh, you have heard that the donut is going away? It may be changing, but we suspect that some form of the donut will survive.)

3. Prepare your one-page medical history

The One Page Medical History
It is a simple fact of arithmetic that the longer you live, the more things that can go wrong with you. What that means is that with every passing year, it will take longer and longer to fill out those endless forms that every doctor requires on your first visit. Moreover, as more things go wrong, there is no way to remember exactly when,

where, and why they went wrong, let alone remembering *in the doctor's office* to list them all.

Finally, these problems will only increase with electronic records because, at this point, we keep seeing all too many doctors preparing their own *(independent)* set of electronic records. This approach will, of course, negate a major positive of having electronic records, such as having one and only one version of your medical history in stored data. This fact makes it all the more important that you carry one version which is correct.

In addition, we have also noticed that when centralized electronic records are presented to a new provider, key information sometimes gets lost in the long lists of health information. We know of the case where the new physician failed to note a history of cancer. Given the way the electronic information was displayed, this outcome was not entirely surprising.

A few years ago we found a simple solution: It is a one-page medical summary of your life. Given the observation above, **use of a one page summary is both a matter of convenience and safety.** The two of us have one-pagers that look very different, but they both contain, often in reverse chronological order:

- **Very Important: Allergies**
  Important: If the allergy is on the sheet, there's a better chance you will remember to mention it.

- **A list of current problems.**
  Include items such as back problems or migraines, again with dates the problem began, doctors, and current treatment.

  • *Type 2 Diabetes* {Melinda ABC, MS NP, xxx- xxx-xxxx}.
  • Diagnosed May, 2010. NovoLog 70/30 twice/day.

- **A way to highlight changes in the course of treatment.**
  Include history/changes in medications for heart patients and others with significant chronic problems.

• *Type 2 Diabetes* {John XYZ, M.D., xxx- xxx-xxxx}
• 10/2003: A1C of 7.2. Subsequent readings of 6.4-6.9 with weight loss.

• **A way to highlight *past* problems of significance.**
  Include items such as pregnancies, heart problems, cancer, significant hospitalizations – with dates, physician in charge, outcomes and current treatment. Get details from copies of tests.

  • *Hospitalization: Fever* {John XYZ, M.D., xxx- xxx-xxxx}.
  • 7/12/07-7/19/07: Fever of 103.
    Tests included brain MRI, Lung CT Scan with dye, EKG, Echocardiogram, Colonoscopy, Sonogram, two GI CT Scans with dye, with only finding of inflammation in lower right GI quadrant/not appendix. Treated with Flagil and two other antibiotics. (CT Chest, Abdomen, Pelvis w/ & w/o contrast, 10/12/2009, mostly unremarkable, Thyroid up-take/scan 11/20/2009 normal.).

  • *L5-S1 Left Disc Herniation* {Tom XYZ, M.D., xxx- xxx-xxxx}.
  • 3/73: L5-S1 left disc herniation, result of athletic injury 3/73.
    Treated at the time solely with traction.

  • *6/27/07: MRI for lower back pain.*
    L3/L4, L4/L5, and L5/S1 all show bulging discs. L3-L4: 50% reduction in spinal canal/L4/L5: 30-50% reduction.

• **A list of all prescriptions and over-the-counter medications and vitamins.**
  Include enough information for a hospital physician to pre-scribe.

> • *Medications: NovoLog 70/30 2x daily; Bisoprolol/HCTZ 2.5 mg/6.25 mg; Restasis (dry eye)*
>
> • *Daily Vitamins/Etc: Vitamin C 500 mg; Calcium/Magnesium/Zinc/Vitamin D supplement; 1 oz. dark chocolate for BP*

• **Pertinent family history.**

Note that in order to provide the most usable information you will need copies of important medical tests. These tests belong to you and you have a right to a copy of all tests. You can get these from your physician or hospital simply by asking.

Caveat: Make sure you keep the summary to one page. Think of it as a resume – any longer and no one will read it. A copy for each of us is kept in our billfolds, with back-up copies somewhere easy to put hands on in any emergency. (Believe me. I have been here, and you do not have time to hunt down this information when three EMS guys are coming up the front walk.)

The really good doctors have thanked us profusely for this short-form summary. In addition, we have found our summary particularly useful:

• **In the emergency room when getting a list of current medications.**

Fast response is really important here and none of us can spell most of those medications.

• **With the doctor who was getting used to the new electronic record-keeping.**

The doctor missed the fact she had a patient with a previous history of abnormal blood tests because that information was way far down in the electronic records and the initial interview had been done by an assistant, not the doctor.

• **With every new doctor's visit.**

Also used whenever current doctor A needs to know about problems handled by current doctor B.

Prescriptions and Vitamins Need to Go in the Budget

If we did not make the point obvious enough above, we need to repeat that vitamins and prescriptions are really expensive and fewer are covered by Medicare Part D than we would like. Do not forget to make a budget line for these when making your housing plans.

Communicating With the Doctor Quickly

What you all know by now is that when you visit your doctor, you are going to get all of 15-20 minutes with that doctor. Further, in the intensity of the moment it is so easy to forget one of the things you meant to ask about. We have also found a ½ page agenda of *things to discuss* to be really useful – one copy for us and one for the doctor. (Make it less than ½ page if possible.)

While you are there, also make sure to have the doctor go over all the prescriptions on your one-pager to make sure you still need all of the prescriptions.

Treating Multiple Medical Problems

What we have not covered may be the single most frustrating aspect of medical care as one gets older. That is the problem of multiple medical problems, i.e., there are two or three things wrong with you, more or less. It is probably more, but we are not going to be picky.

One example of multiple problems is a group of conditions that tend to occur together just because you are older: bad backs, degenerative disk disease, hip arthritis, bulging disks, and spinal stenosis. Another example is metabolic syndrome – a cluster of conditions that increase the risk for coronary artery disease, stroke, and Type 2 Diabetes. These conditions include increased blood pressure, high blood sugar level, excess body fat around the waist, and abnormal cholesterol. The University of Kentucky Healthcare lists common diseases for those with multiple medical problems: diabetes, lung diseases, high blood pressure, heart disease, cancer, stroke, depression and arthritis.

From the examples, you can see that some multiple problems go together because they affect the same or similar body parts (spinal stenosis and bulging lumbar disks), but other multiple problems occur because the older one is, the more apt one is to have each one of the particular medical problems, such as arthritis *and* heart disease. Finally, some go together because having one predisposes the patient to the other one, such as stomach obesity and Type 2 Diabetes.

The New York Times (Brody, 2011) reports that 2/3 of those 65+ and 3/4 of those 80+ have multiple chronic health conditions. Having three things wrong with you, more or less, is quite common.

Issues occur when treating multiple problem patients. Treating one condition may actually worsen another condition. Even more common, patients end up taking a lot of medications each day. We may not even recognize how these meds interact, particularly if prescribed by multiple physicians. You may be covered for drug interactions if your meds all come from one pharmacy. If you use more than one pharmacy, you need to manage drug interaction risks yourself. (Please note that each of these physicians is going to want to see the patient every few months or so, which also leads to the complaint we have previously mentioned that going to doctors leaves little time to actually retire and do those things you wanted to do.)

Unfortunately, there is little research on how to treat multiple problems. One reason for the lack is the simple fact that few multiple problem patients have exactly the same set of problems. As such, physicians today have to take each patient as an individual case. The one area for success at present seems to be using multi-disciplinary teams for patient care. If you have multiple problems and are near any major medical center using these teams, by all means go for it.

As a patient, you (and also your parents) can help the situation by becoming seriously involved in your own (their own) health care. Know what each physician is doing and what he is prescribing and make sure all the physicians know what everybody else is doing and prescribing – another good reason for the one-pager medical history.

In addition, make sure the physicians know how you are reacting to a new drug. If you feel worse, let them know. If you feel better, let them know. If you cannot seem to see any difference, let them know.

The University of Kentucky Healthcare suggests a series of questions to ask your doctors: "Are two or more doctors going to be involved?" – "Are the doctors experienced working together?" – "How will they coordinate my care?" – And when drugs are involved, "How is this new drug expected to interact with the drugs I am currently taking?"

Finally, one problem apparently all too common at hospitals is admitting the elderly patient (more likely your parents, at this age, than you) and finding out that the major reason they are not feeling well is that they are taking way too many drugs. They may be taking multiple drugs for the same problem – different physicians have not been told what the others are prescribing, and there are many different names for the same/similar medications.

The patient may still be taking drugs that were meant for a one-time condition and are no longer needed. I actually had the neighbor who took the flu drug way beyond when she had gotten over the flu. But then, she did not know what the drug was for. The physician said take; she took. Finally and very frequently, the patient continues taking the old medication when a new one is prescribed. Every time a new drug is prescribed, particularly to your parents, you should show the physician the list of drugs that are currently being taken. And periodically, you should be asking whether each drug is still needed.

A last caveat here: Taking a lot of drugs is not necessarily bad, if they are the right drugs. For those with a serious chronic problem, such as heart disease, it may reasonably take quite a few drugs to cover all the situations. Moreover, for some of the drugs for these chronic diseases, they may be working just fine but show no outside signs. Your physician will know how each drug should react.

Getting the Right Diagnosis

Up to this point, we have talked about a patient actually having all the medical problems attributed to him or her. There is a second situation which is far less common, but extremely frustrating. This is the issue of not getting a correct diagnosis for some problem with a lower incidence because the diagnosis always tends to be for problems with a high incidence among the elderly.

In get real language, regardless of what is wrong – regardless of the problem that is really bothering *you* – the diagnosis will be osteoarthritis. And guess what, chances are good you really do have osteoarthritis. Think of it this way: "Do you know a person in their late sixties who does *not* have at least some degree of osteoarthritis?" The issue with this diagnosis is that it may not lead to addressing the symptom that is really bothering you.

So what does one do? Very simply, one learns to be a very good patient. A very good patient is one who knows their body and can describe succinctly and accurately what is going on. That includes telling exactly where the problem exists *(e.g., three inches above the knee on the front side of the knee),* when it started, when it occurs, how long it occurs, what kind of pain is involved (sharp vs. dull ache), and the degree of pain involved on a 10-point scale. You may want to write down your descriptions on the ½ pager for the doctor's visit.

The best exam I ever heard of and the exam that got down to the right problem, was the one where the physician asked the patient to describe the pain from each of three different problems that she was willing to admit she probably had (think things like bulging disks/bad back and spinal stenosis). The descriptions were all different, i.e., the patient could tell the difference. This fact led the physician to go further with his diagnosis and not stop with the most obvious one.

As another example, one way physicians differentiate between rheumatoid arthritis and osteoarthritis is how long in the morning the "stiffness" persists. The better your descriptions, the more likely you will be to experience success.

One issue which arises here is how much you will want to rely on the internet for information. A lot of physicians cringe in terror at the internet-reading patient – especially the one that comes in with a full diagnosis and exact descriptions of the symptoms.

There are two uses of the internet that, personally, we think may be useful. One is to read each description of a new drug prescribed for you to look for interactions and possible bad reactions. (You may want to recheck for drug interactions and side effects every couple of years. The list of drug side effects and interactions can change over time, as one of us learned rather painfully.) A second use is to help in defining what aspects of the medical problem are important to communicate. If the internet helps perfect your descriptions (and does not add symptoms you do not have), then it is probably a good thing. (Do be careful about the old medical student problem where the symptom appears only after the student has read about it, but not before.)

Welcome to the 21st Century
We have talked about Life Alert, the Jitterbug phone, and other communication devices that allow seniors to live safely independent-

ly. Important to our health and safety, however, are not just these devices but the whole digital world in which we now live.

In the fall of 2013, huge floods devastated many of the roads and homes in the canyons going up into the Colorado Rockies. (I described to friends that one of the main roads/highways looked like a giant Cookie Monster had taken a bite right out of the middle of the road.) Homeowners were stranded with no roads to carry them to safety. Needless to say, there was not a lot of electricity. But many kept in touch by using their cell phone to connect to Facebook.

This type of communication is going to happen even more in the future. Motorists and hikers who get lost in the mountains and back woods can now be found using the ping/GPS tracker in their cell phone or car. And I always enjoyed the NCIS episode that used Twitter to "find this plane." The message and a picture of the plane went out to thousands in the area as persons receiving the tweet passed it on to others. The plane was found quickly. Believe it or not, Twitter and crowd sourcing were used recently in the real world to try and find Malaysian Flight 370. Crowd sourced volunteers went over satellite pictures looking for debris.

Net, net, knowing how to use the new social media and their mobile devices may be critical in keeping you safe and healthy at one point or another. If you are a little behind about the intricacies of the modern mobile world, as we have to admit we are, now is the time to upgrade your skills or to tap the grandkids for their expertise.

Chapter 9: Unclutter Our Homes

In Our Dreams

There is a certain point in life when one looks up and says, "I have too much stuff." Amazingly, this is usually an understatement. One very positive aspect of retirement is that, finally, there is time to do something about this nagging problem that all too many of us face. What is even more positive is that uncluttering – if you are about to move to a new abode – has the potential to save you tons of money. (You do not really have to move the 49-piece tea set Great Aunt Elsie gave you which definitely put the finishing touches to your modern décor.)

Get Real Time

We all know there are steps we should take. However, normally following the "I have too much stuff" comment is the inner nudge, "I love my stuff. Please do not take my stuff away. I am sure the kids will want at least some of my stuff." The U.S. Department of Energy has recently reported that 25% of two-car garages are currently <u>not</u> being used to park cars and an additional 32% have room for only one car. Guess what the garages are being used for? The correct answer is not bicycles or ATV's.

One of our Moms actually had this preservation instinct down pat. When she ran out of room in the garage she moved to the front porch. One of her dear friends politely suggested that each person to visit our home should be asked upon leaving to take one item from the porch away with them. The friend figured that would at least provide a good start.

Solutions

About the Kids

We mentioned before that we are not going to spend a lot of time discussing the grandchildren and children. We will hold to that regarding uncluttering. There are simply too many different situations involved to provide simple answers. Each of us has to decide on our own how we are going to approach this very delicate problem of deciding what we do with our stuff, especially regarding the family.

One thing that we all should try to avoid is the situation of a co-worker of one of us. Five years after Grandmother died, the children were still arguing about who was going to get the breakfront and who was going to get the china. If this is a potential problem in your family, you might try any one of a number of solutions – now and not later. Chances are good there will be some hurt feelings, but probably none as bad as five years of arguing over that breakfront.

The most difficult issue regarding uncluttering is deciding what the kids are really not going to want. These items can be sent to auction and may be critical in helping to supplement those retirement savings and saving the kids from having to contribute to your wellbeing. Try asking the kids about items they do not want and promise yourself not to be hurt at some of their answers.

Objectives in Uncluttering

Having a clear set of objectives is the one thing we found most helpful in making those "keep or not" decisions. (We have recently been through two first class unclutterings. Below are two ideas which made the whole experience manageable.)

William Morris, an English interior designer in the late 19th century whose designs are as stunning today as they were 120 years ago, provided us with what may be the single best piece of advice: *"'Have nothing in your house that you do not know to be useful, or believe to be beautiful."* As each item came up, I silently repeated his advice.

We might add a second item to the list. At this point in your life, you will also want to keep a few things (just a few) that you find "meaningful." (For years I kept a navy silk velvet jacket that only fit my younger self but that brought back memories that could not be replaced. It is OK, honest.)

Uncluttering for Retirement

Finally, uncluttering for retirement is somewhat different from the standard uncluttering. No, it is quite different. As we said above, we have been through the "retirement uncluttering" twice now. The first time was to move from the house in city A to a house in city B. The second was to move from the house in city B to an apartment in city C. For the first move, we uncluttered but still took a semi-truck to move our goods. For the second move, we took a truck one-fourth the size of the first to move to the apartment. **We still have too much stuff.**

For retirement moves and unclutterings, there are two objectives. The first is to **organize** those items you are going to need in retirement, with the goal of keeping things simple. This is especially important if a moving van is going to be involved.

The second is to **unclutter** what's left, with the goal of getting the amount of "stuff" down as much as possible. Let us look at each in turn, along with some sub-divisions:

- **Organizing important papers to keep with you at the house or apartment.**

- **Organizing general housekeeping items that should be in easy reach in the new abode.**

- **Organizing important papers for long term storage.**

- **Uncluttering the big items.**

- **Uncluttering all else.**

1. Organizing important papers to keep with you

Before calling upon the "keep, donate, store, and trash" routine, it is really helpful to collect and get in one place a number of items you are going to need and/or will find extremely useful in retirement.

Try putting aside one box or expanding file for each of the following. As you go through the house, move the items below to their anointed box/file. Then make sure the box/file is in an easy place to retrieve. Note: Most of the items below you may have already set aside. Cleaning them out and getting them organized, however, provides the humongous advantage that they are out of the way for the rest of your organizing. You would be amazed at how much clutter disappears when these items are corralled.

Note: As you go through the papers and set aside those out-of-date items to discard, check each for social security numbers. Make sure that those with credit card numbers or social security numbers are **shredded**. We were aghast when we discovered how many documents and receipts, especially those from five to ten years ago, had social security numbers on them. These should be shredded.

- **Charitable receipts needed to document this year's taxes/other papers needed for taxes.**

    Do not forget such items as Goodwill donations, and dues to organizations which allow part to be tax deductible.

- **Medical receipts for this year's taxes.**

    The box will include receipts for Medicare and Part B and D Supplements. You have no idea how many pieces of paper Medicare can generate, but more important, make sure you are saving receipts for uncovered items such as eye glasses or prescriptions only partially covered by the Part D Supplement. Your income will most likely have gone down a lot, so it is easier to make it up to the medical deductible amount.

- **Copies of medical tests.**

  These do belong to you and the source should provide you with copies when asked. You will want a copy as backup to your medical 1-pager plus a copy for new physicians.

- **Receipts for credit cards and all other purchases for the current year.**

- **Copies of internet orders.**

  Keep if you might want to order from this source again, but not for a while. (I did not want to lose the name of the company with high quality, affordable sisal rugs, as well as the color we chose.)

2. Organizing general housekeeping items that should be in easy reach.

Before questioning why this step, just consider for a moment how long it took you to find one AAA battery the last time you needed one. Or better yet, try to uncover the clear wrapping tape with only one trial.

- **Instruction booklets/guarantees.**

  As you already know, these items have the uncanny ability to migrate on their own throughout your house, making them impossible to find the one day you will need them.

- **To go/delivery menus.**

  Your need for these items will be in direct proportion to the degree to which your joints are creaking that day.

- **Maps/travel information.**

  Having maps and brochures ready for that impromptu get away will be most appreciated on that day when you decide to do what retirement is meant for.

- **Gift wrap/mailing materials.**

  Given that the clear wrapping tape is almost as useful as duct tape, this is a good idea to keep handy.

- **Recipes you are honestly going to use.**

- **Coupons you are honestly going to use.**

- **Batteries.**

- **Light bulbs.**

- **Stationery/thank you notes, etc.**

- **Tool kit.**

  Even if you are going to a smaller apartment, you will want to assemble a basic tool kit. A toolkit that can repair (or assemble those items noted as "some assembly required") will still be needed. It has amazed us what we have had to repair (including medical equipment). (On the other hand, the 42-foot extension ladder probably should be sold – see two sections down.)

- **Personal items to keep.**

  These are items you used to put in scrapbooks, but now you just may want to keep. Examples are programs from a grandchild's recitals, or on a sadder note, copies of obituaries for dear friends.

- **Names/addresses.**

  This is a new item. It is one that we both wish we had thought of years ago. Ideally, this box will contain the names of everyone who has ever brushed up against your life – and we mean everyone. (You may want to make copies of the telephone directories for your departments at work and for organizations to which you have belonged.)

The names will be needed for two reasons. The first will come from a desire in retirement or before to make contact with friends from past times. Even more important, the names may be needed when the memory refuses to retrieve the name of someone you knew or worked with before – especially if you might like to use them as a reference, or simply because you will feel better recalling the name.

Regarding the feeling better part, at school, I was part of a group of four students. When I started to think about my group, I was able to recall Mat's name almost immediately. It took two full years to recall Elizabeth's name. I still have no recall of the second guy's name – and we are now talking years of trying.

It is also useful to keep a copy of all your previous addresses with zip code. Amazingly, on more than one occasion some idiot form has demanded my previous addresses from eons ago.

If given a chance, this is a box I would suggest that everyone keep – young and old – especially for networking. If I had started collecting my "names" earlier, I definitely would have consulted the box on many more occasions than I currently have.

Note that your grandchild – off onto the first job, also might find his or her list of "names" to be quite useful later on for career advancement.

3. Organizing important papers for long term storage

These boxes are for long-term storage. You may want to start by using those cardboard file boxes that you buy in bulk at the office supply store. Then, as you get further along, you may want to move the items to plastic filing boxes. These will keep everything dry and safe when stacked in the garage or in the new storage space you are renting.

Note that we have not listed all of the items one needs to save, like wills and birth certificates. Naturally, those need to be organized and saved, also. Below are items which take up room/need a box and which also tend to be scattered around the house.

- **Tax records.**

  Save the tax forms plus back-up documents for that year's taxes. USA.gov (2014) recommends saving each year's taxes for 7 years from the filing date.)

- **Receipts for home purchase/home improvements.**

  You will need these for tax purposes when you sell the home – that may be some time in the future.

- **Supporting tax information for self-employed.**

  Save for 7 years if you are self-employed or own your own business.

- **Investment records.**

  GoodHousekeeping.com (n.d.) recommends keeping as long as you own, plus seven years. At seven years, they go in with the tax records.

- **Papers to keep from**
  - Birth through high school/college/grad school,
  - First two jobs,
  - Other jobs.

  These boxes are for items you *really* want to keep. Try to get everything you want to save into one box for each of these three periods (or other periods you select). This will force you to only keep the good stuff. (You may also want to make up a box for each grandchild.)

- **Yearly Receipts – One Box/ Year.**

  You will want to keep all receipts for a given year for a period of seven years.

4. Uncluttering the big items

Before we just threw out things that we knew we did not need. This part is a little harder. We have a new objective. As you come across each item, ask yourself, "Would someone else like this better/use this more than I would?" (*Was this item never your style? Does this item seem to scream "for old people"?*) If the answer is "yes" to any of the above, the only question is whether it might be more appropriate (i.e., make you more money) to place the item at auction or in a yard/garage sale or whether it would be better to just donate it to charity.

- **Furniture.**

  Friends of ours were packing for the big move and they kept tripping over the furniture. The furniture was in fairly good shape but it also had drawbacks as they got older. Their "old life" furniture consisted of really big, really heavy couches and other massive furniture pieces. The furniture they wanted for their "new life" would be light, easily moved by a 70 year-old to clean/rearrange, and easily/inexpensively moved to yet another home/destination.

  A few of those big "old life" furniture pieces got sent to auction, along with family heirlooms (see Chapter 3) and a lot of unused stuff. Happily, our friends used their auction proceeds to purchase a few pieces which basically updated their whole décor while providing lighter/easier to move pieces. As an aside, one replacement for heavier pieces they really love was black wire shelving that can be disassembled for a move and yet will look good in any room.

- **Books.**

  This should be a quickie. Basically, if this is not a book you are going to refer to in the future for any one of a number of reasons or read again in part or in whole because it had meaning for you and your life, it should go in the box for the local book sale or be given to the local library.

• **Tools.**

Maybe, just maybe in your new abode you will not need that leaf blower, mower, snow blower, tree trimmer, along with table saws, chain saws, tools, etc. These items can bring *a lot of money* to supplement those retirement savings, once you have separated out the basic tool kit to save. Your local experience, however, will help you decide whether to put out the rest of the tools at your own garage/yard sale or whether to place them at a local auction (and pay a small commission.)

• **Family Heirlooms.**

We covered much of this in Chapter 3, but as a review: silver (in almost any form) is good for bringing in funds for the retirement savings, especially in the hands of a good auctioneer. To repeat, trying to lose the family china, however, will not be easy. You will keep hearing these words, "Kids today just do not want the family china." This will be even truer if that beautiful gold or silver band around your china cannot become best friends with a dishwasher or microwave. Finally, look carefully at your "collections" – those items you have picked up along the way and on your travels. Some may surprise you and really be worthwhile. (We had people at auction picking up some handmade jewelry for more than we could go out today and purchase new.)

5. Uncluttering all else

Hopefully by now, you are beginning to see some empty spaces in your home that you have not seen in a long time. Now we get down to the regular, old organizing and uncluttering. This requires four boxes or piles:

• **Items you want to keep (but just need to put away where they belong).**

• **Items to give away or sell.**

• **Items to be stored (perhaps in your new rented storage space).**

• **The trash pile.**

When you finish this portion of the uncluttering, you are allowed to breathe a sigh of relief, to feel as if the world has been moved off your shoulder, and to really prep you mind for that retirement ahead. Go for it!

Chapter 10: UnCluttering Our Minds

In Our Dreams

Many of us have envisioned retirement as a time for being able to think about things a little beyond the necessities of everyday life. We will finally have time to consider why we are here and where the world is going and what is the true meaning of life.

Get Real Time

Unfortunately what we found is that instead of delving into the existential questions of life, we seem to have been really busy thinking about something else. You will likely end up there also. *(This topic is not the most uplifting of all we will cover. But it is very important.)*

A little way into retirement, you will most likely find yourself going over – no, obsessing over – events from your past life. And unfortunately, you will find that you tend to spend an inordinate amount of time on events that were not necessarily the most pleasant. And yet you keep going back to those events – again and again. And you keep doing this.

Solutions

Reliving Your Life – A Necessity

Both of us have found ourselves obsessed with some past events we ought to just drop. But we are also coming to the conclusion that at least some of this may be a necessary part of getting on to the next station in life. There is psychological research showing that people tend to remember tasks that were unfinished because they were interrupted. We are thinking that some of these memories are like unfinished tasks. They need to be brought up and discussed with ourselves so we can adopt a more finished way of thinking about them.

We have concluded in a couple of cases that we simply have to accept the fact that not everyone is a nice person and some were downright mean. But if we can get to a conclusion like this, we can pack up that event and store it in the "finished" category. (Believe this – those people are not going to get "nicer" if we think about them more.)

There are other events where I may have been the klutz, the idiot, the non-thinking one, the only senior who fell flat on her face in front of the principal while doing a polka. (Yes, it happened.) Unfortunately, I cannot go back and change the past now, but I can resolve to pack this one up and just not do something like this in the future.

There is also a very nice part to these remembrances. You will also have time to think about the really nice events from the past. One day when really down, I picked up a pen and wrote down the experiences I really remember as "great." It is a wonderful thing to do. As a simple example, somehow I will never forget one hot summer night in July in Colorado Springs, CO, when the air had that chill that only comes from the high mountains. We stood in front of our motel room and watched cars go by with the snow-capped mountains in the background. I will never forget it. Simple as can be.

What you need to know, we think, and this is a personal observation, is that going over the past may just be very normal. It may also be the reason that there is so much advice about interacting with others: Your socializing keeps you from getting obsessed about these sad thoughts. And remember, you yourself can always change the topic of your thoughts to the good and proud times.

Keeping that Brain Well-Exercised
Beyond much else, one of the absolutely most frustrating parts about growing older is "losing" one's memory. For the life of you, you cannot remember the name of that old friend – that person who was your best friend for ten years. You cannot remember the name of that

hotel you loved so much on your first wedding anniversary. You cannot even remember the name of the doctor who delivered your first born child. Is it not amazing that you cannot forget all those times when you made a fool of yourself, but you cannot remember the name of your best friend from high school? It is simply amazing.

Yes, it is frustrating not to be able to remember things you should be able to recall on a moment's notice. Never fear: there is great news just released. The Journal of Topics in Cognitive Science (Knapton, 2014) has recently released research showing that we have not forgotten; we just take longer to remember. The researchers maintain that the brains of the elderly are slow because they know so much. The brains of the elderly only "appear" to slow down because they have so much information. It is much like a full-up hard drive on a computer. The brains of the elderly are not weak. They simply know more and take longer to access the information.

Now about that frustration: we have a suggestion that seems to work for us. You might try it. Earlier psychological research has shown that memory depends on recency and frequency: the more recent a memory, the better the retrieval; the more frequent a memory, the better the retrieval.

Let us say you are trying to recall the name of the actor in *Bullitt,* Steve McQueen. Try remembering everything you can that surrounds the actor. He starred in the movie with filmdom's best ever car chase. He died of cancer at an early age in Mexico. The movie was filmed in San Francisco. He also starred in *The Great Escape* and *The Thomas Crown Affair*. He took on the persona of the anti-hero during the time of the Vietnam War.

Back to remembering: The theory here is that you are stimulating other memories that also may be stored with McQueen's name, some of which may be easier to retrieve (or will help others retrieve the name for you.)

P.S. If you do not know who Steve McQueen is, you are too young to be reading this book. If you know who Steve McQueen is and he is a British film director born in 1969, you are also too young to be reading this book, but you are very much up to date.

We do have one suggestion: when you cannot remember, instead of dredging up that worn-out "senior moment" phrase, try the following, "I stored that piece quite a while back. It is going to take a while to retrieve."

We have two final words on this topic. First, we both have had times when it took as much as a week or two to uncover the name we were trying to retrieve. After not even considering the question for days, all of a sudden the name will pop up out of the blue. It is our guess that the brain has been working on the problem the entire time, probably during "down time" when we aren't thinking about something else. These very long term retrievals are usually for someone you worked with thirty or forty years ago.

Second, we are talking here about human long term memory. This is not the same thing as Alzheimer's disease. Alzheimer's is very different and is also very serious. For our memory example, a normal sign of aging might be to forget where you left the keys. A sign of Alzheimer's might be (but not definitely) leaving the keys in an inappropriate place, such as the refrigerator. A normal sign of aging might be forgetting details of a conversation. Alzheimer's might be forgetting that the conversation occurred. Normal aging might be forgetting to write a check. Alzheimer's might be losing the ability to manage a checkbook altogether. If symptoms like the Alzheimer's ones occur in a loved one, seek medical advice.

Chapter 11: Things to Do and other Secrets of a Happy Retirement

In Our Dreams

So far we have looked at retirement from a number of different perspectives: health, safety, where to live, whether to buy, how to remain financially secure, etc. There remains one gaping hole in our narrative, and that is how we approach retirement to assure ourselves that we can make it a happy one. Answering that question required research.

So there we were, mere pilgrims on our way to discovering the world and the secrets of a happy, successful retirement. We knew with conviction that if we really put our minds to it, we would be successful in our mission. We scoured the internet to uncover the knowledge of others. Our quest would be never ending. And we did come away with a number of observations.

1. Those writing about retirement have mostly not been there.
Just take a look at the pictures of many of the *amazingly young* authors of various blogs, articles, and books on the topic of retirement. And note not only how similar their suggestions are to each other but also to previously written descriptions of retirement for earlier generations, especially the Greatest Generation. (You will see below that we Boomers are not necessarily like earlier generations.)

2. Several ideas did seem to pop up regardless of the source.
We found the following suggestions for happiness in *many, many* of the retirement guides we examined. We present these ideas to keep you on your toes and to make sure you are well versed in the subject. Of course, we are not sure that all of these suggestions refer to a lot of us as Baby Boomers, but it cannot hurt to see what other folks say.

- **For a happy retirement, sign up your brain for exercise class.**

*Research (Lazar, 2014) reported in the Journal of the American Geriatrics Society showed long-lasting results from brain exercises. Three quarters of those who participated in reasoning exercises and information-processing drills displayed these abilities a decade later. According to the authors, these long-lasting effects from the brain exercises may indicate a **potential for possibly** delaying dementia or attenuating it.*

"Need to exercise our brains"

"Keep mind sharp"

"Work brain cells"

"Work your mind"

"Keep brain stimulated"

"Learn something new"

Note: As we write this, we are looking for an exercise class for our brains. Let us know if you find one. (OK. Not kidding. It is most likely the case that keeping the brain active and working is an excellent idea.)

- **For a happy retirement, travel the world.**

"Travel"

"Collect experiences to enrich your life"

"See the world, be on the move"

"Focus on the journey"

"Travel – travel"

Yes, our grandparents did want to see the world. However, that was before the TSA and body checks made air travel such fun. That was before cruise ships stopped regularly in mid-ocean for a relaxing tow back to shore. That was before most of our TV series were being shot across the world so, when we travel, we can note how much real life looks like the pictures. (We Boomers love travel, but we probably will not do it the same way as the grand folks.)

• **For a happy retirement, volunteer, keep active.**
"Be an agent of change"
"Keep active"
"Give back"
"Volunteer"
Our favorite line here is from a very successful 91-year-old retiree. "Keep involved with others, even if you have to volunteer." (Do not let him kid you. He did far more than his fair share of giving back. But to be honest, his thought frequently mirrors ours.)

• **And finally, several sources have summed it up:**
"Save enough to last throughout your retirement"
"Stay healthy"
"Keep active"
And now that we know how easy it is to accomplish the three items above, we can go party. OK??

Get Real Time

When we look at the retirement of our folks and grand folks, we tend to see travel (lots of travel), golf (much golf), arts and crafts, a lot of scrapbooking, a lot of quilt making, book groups, card groups, keeping organizations going (such as a retired teachers group, a town's historical society, etc.), and finally lots of exercise classes (swimming, yoga, senior exercises, etc.) with the treat of a trip to Baskin Robbins.

These activities are all good. And let us assure you, they will be around for a long time to come. However, we are Baby Boomers. We have put our own stamp on everything we have done. There is no reason to think that retirement will be any different. **We Boomers will do retirement – our way**.

For example, when we look at our Boomer friends who have already retired, we will need a few replacements. (Note: these are real observations – not made up for this section):

• **About those card groups, try replacing canasta/pinochle with Sudoku or with Words with Friends from Facebook where your friends may be a thousand miles away**

• **Replace actual quilt making with a virtual quilt on Pinterest – gathering pictures you love in an area of interest.**

• **Replace arts & crafts with some photo finishing on Instagram or uploading your newest YouTube creation or adding another item to your Facebook wall.**

• **Replace geriatric swim exercises with a session at Curve or other fitness center or replace with biking up the mountain or kayaking across the lake.**

• **Replace the ice cream with a dinner at the new Nepalese restaurant.**

Yes, we really are different. And we will redefine great retirements like no one has envisioned before. And when we finally join those at the nursing home, you can bet that our digital world will have produced something to keep us busy – beyond anything we can conjure up now.

How We Differ From Earlier Retirees

It is not just the presence of digital/mobile/laptops/pc's in our lives that has caused our activities to change. Think about these:

• **We look younger; we act younger; in reality we are younger (65 really is the new 50).**

• **Back in the 80's they were asking whether we would still be wearing jeans when we got "old."**

The real question is – have we ever been known to wear anything else???

• **Back in the 80's they feared we would never drink coffee again.**

Thank the world for my double Latte.

• **Mom and her cohorts kept their Elizabeth Taylor hair (short, tight curls) up to the very end.**

Some of us, on the other hand, have short hair. Some have long. Some hair is gray. Some is not.

• **Our daughters shop for ethnic food at the organic grocery.**

We shop for ethnic food at the organic grocery.

• **Mom was secretary at the historical society.**

Depending on our bent, we are on the college alumni board setting educational policy or we are the treasurer for the Kayaking Society.

• **Mom fixed a casserole to take to the pot luck.**

We are fixing a four-course Indian meal for a few friends.

• **Our grandparents toured Europe.**

While we still love travel, we are more apt to jump in the car and make our way cross country touring the backwoods.

Solutions

In our Solutions section, we are going to look at things to do from several different perspectives. Take your pick and may you never be bored. We are going to present loads of ideas, but even this many will only touch the surface of things to do. Try using these suggestions as a way to fire up your creative juices.

Words of Wisdom From One Who Has Been There
We spoke earlier about a few words from a retiree in his nineties. He obviously is not a Boomer, but his words are worth listening to.

Stay active. That has been most important and has really helped me. Socialize with family and friends. I joined a senior citizens group and became their official greeter. Keep up with your hobbies and stay active. Enjoy life and keep a sense of humor. Do not be those people with nothing to do who complain all the time that they are unhappy.

And you know, our friend is a pretty happy fellow. He is also in pretty good health, takes few medications, does his own laundry (the washer and dryer are on the main floor in the kitchen), and cooks his own food. And maybe most important of all – a lifelong actor – he is still acting in the local theatre and still loves every minute of it.

Things to Do – At the Senior Center, At the Newcomer's Club
Some of the best suggestions we found were looking at activities at local senior centers and local newcomer's clubs. We highly suggest that these two can be really helpful in making retirement enjoyable.

• **Hiking and Biking**
Bicycles, motorbikes, hiking, railfanning (exploring railroads and the industries they serve)

• **Dining**
Dinner and a movie with another couple/dinner and a movie with those from the senior center/dinner for 8 (four couples take turns fixing dinner for the other three)/brunch with the group/singles dining out/coffee at friends/a large group reserving a bus to a regional restaurant known for its fried chicken or some other delicacy

- **Arts/Music**

  Classical concerts/theatre/tours/wine tasting – group goes to concerts once a month and then meets to discuss the experience

- **Games**

  Bunco/game night at the center/pinochle, not to mention those games with the ability to increase one's income

- **Creative**

  All sorts of creative endeavors – you can do what you wish with others doing what they wish, i.e., Instagram meets Pinterest meets an actual quilt

- **Garden club**

  Great for sharing cuttings and seeds

- **Volunteering**

  Not only for other seniors' needs but for kids, the needy, etc.

- **And our favorite: ALIVE from one town's newcomer's club**

  The ALIVE group provides for its members Absolutely Lacking Intrinsic Value Entertainment. (They meet every so often for a casual lunch.)

Lots of Other Things to Do

Below is a randomly ordered list of other things to do. There is one rule. Do something you really like. Remember: "Retirement is when we pay ourselves to do the things we love."

- Learn to paint
- Take voice lessons
- Take dance lessons – especially the Argentinian Tango
- Write a book
- Volunteer at the art museum
- Volunteer at a pre-school
- Act in a play

THINGS TO DO FOR A HAPPY RETIREMENT

- Sing in the city Chorale
- Do the props and scenery for a play
- Do the costuming for a play
- Volunteer at the zoo
- Volunteer at the raptor conservatory
- Volunteer at the hospital gift shop
- Start a blue grass festival
- Travel to a blue grass festival
- Sew the dress you always wanted to have
- Explore your family's ancestry
- Explore the country of your family's ancestry
- Write a piece on the city's history
- Participate in five 5K runs
- Learn a new language
- Learn a new computer language – try Ruby on Rails or Python
- Make soap and other items with beautiful fragrances
- Make candles
- Go jogging
- Go hiking
- Go hiking in a new state – or country
- Make a snowman
- Become an expert in some esoteric area – such as Navaho vases, antique sugar safes
- Start a garden
- Make crafts with dried flowers
- Make homemade Christmas presents
- Offer to give a few talks at the Rose Society
- Volunteer at the Botanical Gardens
- Volunteer at the poverty center
- Volunteer at the senior center
- Learn a new digital game, such as Words with Friends

- Write poetry
- Train a dog
- Train a cat (just kidding, honest)
- Take up jump roping
- Take up hop scotch
- Cook everything in the James Beard cookbook
- Eat everything you cooked from the James Beard cookbook
- Etc., etc.

When the Doing Stops: About Boredom

We have not done a "get real" for this section yet. We do need to do so, because we need to discuss "boredom." One outcome which many not-yet-retirees fear is being bored. They ask themselves, "What will I do when I do not have work anymore? Can I really play golf or cards or travel or watch ballgames every day?"

Fortunately, we can say, "Never fear." Retirement has many, many parts to it.

1. First is simply carrying on the everyday activities that have always been there

Grocery shopping, big box shopping, walking the dog, cooking, cleaning, caring for the garden, car maintenance, etc. (Already we are keeping you busy – maybe unhappy but not bored.)

2. Second are those activities that are now much more frequent because you are getting older

Doctor's appointments, picking up prescriptions, exercise classes and/or time in the fitness room, etc.

3. Third is time for refreshing and uncluttering the mind – that is, reorganizing and re-packaging past memories both good and bad. (See the previous chapter.)

This may include a physical aspect, such as finishing the family scrapbook or updating Facebook entries. Early on in retirement, uncluttering will also include house and home uncluttering, to organize the physical life for the retirement to come. Believe it or not, the house uncluttering was one part I really enjoyed because it brought up a lot of good memories and left me with a great sense of accomplishment.

4. Finally, time needs to be cleared for the fun and involving activities you planned on before you retired.
It is funny and strange that often the fun/involving activities get lost in the other parts of retirement. One complaint heard loud and clear is that doctors and health care are taking up so much time that the fun parts of retirement get short changed. (Unfortunately, we do not have a good solution for this at present, particularly if one is also acting as a caretaker. Hopefully in the future we will devise more efficient ways to handle retiree healthcare.)

When you do get free for the fun/involving activity, the next question is, "What activity?" Early on in retirement we thought that many of our friends were, in fact, bored. Their boredom also seemed to come as a surprise to them. We noted that our friends seemed to move from activity to activity and did not seem to be happy with any one of their choices. As time went on, however, we found that each of them slowly but surely moved into an area which they presumably liked.

Of interest, the friends who seemed most at ease were ones who were exploring their more creative sides, whether it was designing an Instagram page or painting or writing or continuing to explore the world or doing something that had been prevented during their working years. Others who seemed equally at ease were those out supporting a cause in which they strongly believed – including carrying a picket sign and passing the word that funds were needed.

For each of us that fun/involving activity will be different. Hopefully, however, for each of us it will be a topic that truly turns us on. And that folks is why we have no expectation of being bored.

Chapter 12: Finale

Make a Job and Even More Secrets to a Happy Retirement

In Our Dreams

In addition to living less expensively, a lot of us are going to want to work. Continuing to work has numerous advantages, not the least of which is having somebody to have lunch with – and on a regular basis to boot. Working will keep the brain nimble, and you may even learn new things. Working will even keep the body nimble, especially if you use lunch hour for a quick run or walk. Finally, working provides friends to talk to, if only to grouse about – yes, work.

Get Real Time

Normally, our "Get Real Time" section forces us to confront some of the not so nice things about where our dreams will take us. (And we could do that here, but then you already know about jobs and workers over 60). So instead, we are going to take a very, very positive view here. We are going to maintain that – with a little creativity, we all can make a job we are going to love!

Wait a minute – you are noting to yourself that we did not say "find" a job; we said "make" a job. Remembering that "retirement is when you pay yourself to do something you love," all we need to do is explore that area of doing something we love. Once we have found it, we can "make" a job out of our passion. Here goes!

One little note. Being retired gives one a great advantage here. When making a job, at the beginning we may want to try out our skills on a "free" basis for some of our friends. When we were younger, we could not do this because it meant giving up the paying job. But now, because we will have some other sources of income, we can try out quite a few different approaches. As we develop the job further, we can then start to charge for our services.

Please note that many of those high tech hot stocks today are still looking to find a source of revenue. We loved the comment the other day, "The only trouble with Facebook is that it has little E to go with its P and E."

Solutions

Where Are You an Expert???

The first area we will explore is areas where you are an expert. If you are an expert, you can pass that information on to someone else. You may want to try out your teaching skills by offering your wisdom for free, but if you are good at it, soon you can offer to let your students pay. Again, look at our list below as a mere start for some real creative thinking about jobs you could make.

Think about jobs you have held.

- **Fix my Website … Please.**

  If you have web development skills, take a look at the websites (and also Facebook pages) in your local area. Particularly look at restaurants and other retail outlets. Note how many of these websites are out-of-date. Better yet, find one that is up-to-date. (Best of luck.) And it is no surprise. It is not atypical for web development companies to charge a couple of thousand or more to do a website for a local business. What is not always clear is the large amount they will tend to charge should you ever want to change that website – like the restaurant who would like to tell you they have a new spring menu.

You might examine a web updating service. With some ingenuity, program pieces can be written to make changing a site very easy. The trick is not to charge your client a fortune for every little change, but instead to charge in such a way that it encourages changes to be made and made often.

• **Mentor on Computerized Equipment.**
Companies are screaming today that they cannot find workers with the skills they need. If you listen carefully, you will find that many of the loudest screamers are those with digital equipment that needs to be programmed and maintained. A very large number of production lines these days are run by computerized equipment. Because many company higher-ups and HR personnel do not understand how to make them work, they try to hire persons already trained on that exact machine. But that does not work because each machine is a little different and chances are the prospective employee has had experience on a similar but not identical computerized piece of equipment.

If you are trained, however, you could offer your previous company some kind of arrangement to train some possible hires, particularly those with experience on similar machines.

Note: We personally find it abominable that so many U.S. companies do not train their employees in technical skills. Other countries can – particularly Germany. In other words, we do not sympathize with these executives when they say they cannot find skilled workers. These companies could and should use the skills of their newly retired staff.

The real question is where such a position might take you. With a little experience in the mentoring business, you can open up a training center where you can make even more money.

- **Mentor for Guys and Gals in the Neighborhood.**

  How are you at fixing leaking faucets? How are your carpentry skills? Are you an expert in furniture refinishing? Have you practiced good interior design on your own for years? Could you stage a house for sale? Did you just finish uncluttering/organizing your house? What do you know about federal guidelines on historic preservation? What do you know about antique shopping? What do you know about …?

  For years, we traveled to the West for vacation and somewhere along the way we would always pick up a souvenir or two, especially jewelry, a vase, art, or handmade goods. I was exceedingly surprised, one afternoon, to discover that my knowledge on uncovering a particular type of fake was quite a bit above that of the souvenir store owner. If you are truly interested in an area, you probably know enough to pass that expertise along to friends (for free at first), to members of an interest club (like the local gem society) and later to the neighborhood/city/town (for a nominal fee). And down the line, you can consider a real, profit-making business, such as House Staging or House Organizing or Basic Plumbing. (For all of these ideas, you may also want to check out needed licenses and also talk with a good law firm (or Legal-Zoom.com) and have them help you draw up some releases so no one is suing you later.)

- **Have you found the 21st Century?**

  We have talked a lot about 21st century digital skills, such as using a mobile phone, finding apps for the phone or tablet, texting, using Facebook safely, Pinterest basics, etc. And – do not tell anyone, there are areas here where the two of us are seriously deficient. I mean seriously. We have talked about hiring a teen to teach us the basics. However, I bet there are some of you out there who also have these skills and could pass them on to your cohorts. And I bet a lot of us would pay you for the privilege.

- **Have you found the 20th Century?**
  We spent much of our adult life in St. Louis. The University of Missouri at St. Lois had and still has a marvelous program to teach computer skills, such as Access, Word, Excel, PowerPoint, and to teach programming for languages like Java, C#, Visual Basic, etc. What has been frightening is to learn how difficult it is in other towns to get this type of training without signing up for a degree. We learned one day to our deep surprise that a group of high school kids in our town had formed an after-school club to *teach themselves* Java, a major programming language.

  We really can use more ways to get a digitally literate young adult base. If you know these programs, you can really help. You can start by mentoring on a one-to-one basis and move later on to small classes, both of which can bring in income.

- **Mentor/Programmer for Specialized Computer Programs**
  What specialized computer programs do you know? This area has functioned as the Catch 22 for many, many IT personnel. The job description for a lot of IT jobs starts out with a list of 5-10 different skill sets/languages that the applicant must know. Many, if not most, IT sophisticated retirees have experience in these areas. Then, hidden down at the bottom of the list, is some esoteric program written especially for that industry or company and not used outside those areas.

  What non IT executives need to know is that most software personnel can pick up a new language/program with a couple of weeks experience. You could either make an offer to your previous company to mentor possible new hires on the program *or* you could offer to take a new job and learn on the job with a low salary to begin with, which would rise with your experience. And with experience, like above, you can start your own training center.

• **Were you a manager?**

The other screamers among those looking for personnel are those who claim that "kids today just do not have any management skills. They do not know even simple things like email etiquette. They do not know how offices work." Here is an area where the target market for your mentoring might be the millennials (18-33 year-olds) who want a step up in their job search. And their parents (whose basement bedroom is currently being occupied) might just be willing to pay for your knowledge in order to free up a guest room.

• **Is there an easier way?**

Most of what we have suggested above requires that you put together and organize the services you are going to provide. Fortunately, the 21st century is providing internet apps which provide the organization for you – at least in some cities so far with more to come, we are sure. For example, you can rent out one of your rooms (via Airbnb), you can offer to drive folks to their destinations in your car (via Uber, Lyft, and Sidecar), you can offer to carry out maintenance and other tasks like pet sitting (via TaskRabbit and Fiverr), you can deliver groceries (via Instacart), etc., etc. We call this the sharing economy, the peer economy, and/or the gig economy. Go for it…it is added income!

• **Do you know how to program a mobile phone or mobile apps?**

Do not worry about this one. We hear that should you have those skills, you are in great demand and probably are already at work. If you have never heard of Python, Ruby with Ruby on Rails, or Objective C you can proceed to the next section.

Jobs Needing Creativity

• Make Something You Cannot Find.

One of the problems with products today is that too much of the stuff we purchase looks alike. It is really difficult to find unique clothing, in particular. If you can sew, however, you can make those items. And if you like them, you might find that your friends might like these items too.

I remember a caftan made from all cotton that had been permanently pleated and was gathered around the neckline. It had a tropical design, so it looked more like a dress than a robe. Plus, it packed into nothing for a trip. Oh what I would not give to have that caftan back. Another item, very hard to find, is a towel wraparound for after the shower. That one is easy to make.

Get a friend to bring by the pants they really love the fit on. You can cut a pattern from the well-fitting pants and make them another pair.

And so on and so on. And that is only for clothes.

• Creative Lectures.

In Korea, the kids have to take a series of exams at the end of school. These exams are important in determining where they end up in life. Of interest to us in the U.S., what the kids have to study with are CD-ROMs with mini-lectures on specific topics which will appear on the tests. They cost about the same as a music CD.

Since these CD-ROMs are all for sale, the best sales go to the lecturers who are most exciting and most illuminating for the tests. Apparently the best lecturers are seen almost as celebrities, in the same realm as rock stars. Gee, it would really be great if we could have exciting learning venues!

To provide a very simple example, say one is giving a lecture on a certain artist. To give life to the lecture, one could add a local artist to illustrate particular techniques. If the topic is gravity, one could have the lecture on a 20th floor balcony and run the gravity experiment as part of the lecture. If one is talking about Greek history, one could add a film touring the Parthenon. Whatever. Whatever. Lots of things can be done to make a lecture truly interesting. You can start by placing a short film on YouTube and move later to making money with your lectures.

• **Advertising Creativity for Online and Mobile – Please.**
If you have an interest in the stock market, you may have noticed the large number of recent IPO's (Initial Public Offerings) for new companies that do not seem to have any source of income beyond selling stock or at least not a large source. This was true of Facebook for a long time and is true of all too many new offerings such as Twitter. It seems that the best anyone has done so far with many of these online and mobile applications is to throw some Google ads at the website or mobile page. (Currently, online/mobile advertising does not return as much to advertisers as advertising in typical mass media.)

You may have noticed some of the typical Google ads. Many consist of small boxes with 8-10 words in the box. (For example: Get Men's Cotton T-Shirts in Great Colors & Styles. Order Now!) The creativity is simply underwhelming, she said snoring. Other, non-Google ads simply show the product being sold. As a result, too many of us have learned how to "turn off" seeing the right-hand side of web pages so we literally don't even see many of these ads.

Of interest, many 21st century web/mobile ads are very reminiscent of the copy that used to appear in catalogs for retail outlets like Macy's. (Oh yes, we are referring to the 1940's. Many of Madison Avenue's finest creative personnel in the 20th century started by writing copy for store catalogs.)

Retail advertising for television and radio long ago moved beyond catalog copy. (Note some of the really fine Christmas television ads for the top retail outlets this season.) There are two major steps to developing today's outstanding advertising. The first major step to high level creative is finding a way to "position" a product in consumers' minds so that they want to purchase. Hallmark Cards wanted to position their greeting cards as the highest quality. Creative minds then went to work to find the best way to carry that positioning out. They came up with the tagline, "When you care enough to send the very best." The second major step for Hallmark was to use the creative personnel to develop and produce a fine set of executions portraying "when you care enough to send the very best." That positioning/tag line has been in use now for more than half a century.

The real question is why online/mobile advertising cannot be more like the rest of today's advertising. There is no reason today why mobile and web advertising has to be dull or small or unobtrusive or dumb. Looking only at the graphics, websites of course have the capability of showing film. We could do something as simple as finding an enticing way to place a short film into the site, so that consumers will want to see the film rather than "x" their way beyond it. Or we could experiment with a very wide print ad placed against a stunning landscape. Or we could try something very, very different, such as reserving a whole page of a website for ads only. The field is wide open, and that's for both positioning and for graphics. Help is sorely needed. And interestingly, a potential breakthrough target for creative efforts may well be local retailers.

PostScript: The Future

So far we've looked at the best practices currently available for approaching different aspects of retirement life. As we leave, we would like to look to the future. There are a few areas where improvement is still due – areas which you may not be encountering now, but which will probably crop up as the years go by.

There is a reason we have selected this path to conclude our work. Here is a prime opportunity for retirees to get together with millennials (now ranging in age from 18-33) to provide both with a happiness key to the future. We can solve our own problems and, at the same time, provide some worthwhile experiences or maybe even careers and jobs for our grandchildren.

Example of a Problem Solved

We would like to start by showcasing a simple case, beautifully done, of meeting one need of older seniors. These are not big problems. But these are problems which older seniors will appreciate beyond your wildest dreams when they are solved. The example is in one of the western states county parks. The park follows a mountain stream as it meanders down the canyon. Along the way, the county has built picnic areas and camping areas. You do not tend to see anything but water and trees, but quietly hidden are sidewalks which take one directly to washrooms and beyond that down to picnic tables right above the stream. The wilderness is still there, but now one can be at ease taking great grandma to the picnic in her wheelchair. (It should also be noted that the sidewalks also tend to keep visitors away from the undisturbed natural areas where lots of wildlife live.)

Areas Needing Improvement

Below are examples of some areas where we retirees could use some improvement – at least in some towns and cities:

- **Connection Problems when you no longer drive.**
  By the early age of 65, one in five adults no longer drives. Now, some may simply be New Yorkers or other large city dwellers where driving is less than the most practical way to get from A to B. On the other hand, as the years go by, more and more of us will realize that we need or want to pass that task on to others. A disability may also prompt leaving the driving to others.

  The New York Times recently featured an 80 year-old couple in San Diego who decided to explore how they would cope without the family car (Edleson, 2014). They successfully tried out the Grossmont Trolley System. And their only problem: how did they get the half mile distance from their home to the bus stop???

  We would like to point out that, in our town, the problem not only exists at the start, but also on the destination end, where it is a minimum 2-3 block walk to get from the bus to the area of town with all the fun shops and restaurants.

  A particularly forward-looking town we know of has a beautiful, brand new light transportation system which is completely ADA compliant: No steps to get on the bus. There is plenty of room at the back for, not only bikes, but wheelchairs and walkers – without having to disassemble them. But, for many riders, they too have what we will call "The Connection Problem" on both ends of the line. All is fine once you get to the bus from your home or to the restaurant and shops from the bus. It is in the connecting where the problems start.

  Think about the possibility of a group of millennials (or even younger seniors) getting together and agreeing, for a nominal contribution, to transport older seniors over the connection areas to get them to the trolley/metro-bus/light rail. (This may require permits/insurance/etc.)

- **New Buildings for Older People.**

  In another recent article, the writer describes taking his father to the new medical building, only to discover that the brand new furniture had no arm supports to help his 80-year-old father get up from the seat (Aronson, 2014). We saw this problem first hand in the newly decorated Intensive Care Waiting Room at a local hospital. The room was filled with about 40 beautiful new couches and chairs – with not an arm or arm support in sight. Even we had a problem – not to mention the young mother with baby. The writer goes on to note that all sorts of problems can cause difficulties in mobility, from a "bum" leg to difficulty walking long distances to troubles from hearing loss to young motherhood.

- **Connecting in Outdoor Spaces.**

  Recently, an older sports fan related problems he had getting from the stadium parking lot (grass-covered) to the stadium itself. It is far more difficult than most know getting a walker to "walk" across grass-covered surfaces. Apparently, there are some sidewalks, but they are not always in the right places.

  Note: It is also very difficult to get a walker to navigate thick pile carpets found in places like hotels and theatres.

- **Ahhh, for a Chair to Sit In.**

  A few years ago, one of us was in the traditional big box store – a box which always seems to be a bit bigger than we remember. I asked the manager if it would be possible to judiciously place a sturdy chair or two at the back of the store to help us catch a second breath – a few regularly spaced chairs where people can rest and regroup. The manager mumbled. (My writing partner noted that managers of big box stores aren't always given leeway to change things.) Of interest, right after my request I heard five other shoppers spontaneously start to clap. All those clapping were younger than I am.

Solutions and How to Get There

The main question is how do we uncover needs like these for older seniors? How do we uncover those areas where the simple problems of growing older, such as an inability to walk longer distances, become real handicaps without intervention by us younger ones?

The needs we have listed above are not the sort of thing that the American's with Disabilities Act is always going to cover, nor will the local building folks always think to include such amenities. Yet, more and more of us are going to be forever thankful when one of these problems gets tackled. And if our millennial grandkids can get involved, we may find ways to get them some valuable experiences. For example, as we suggested above, they might consider getting a group together to help seniors with the Connector problem (i.e., getting between home and the bus/public transit and getting between the bus/public transit and the shops and restaurants). Alternatively, those interested in public service careers might work with community boards and hotels and retail outlets, etc., to get sidewalks and chairs and couches in the right places (great for including on resumes).

One way of uncovering needs we haven't talked about comes from a technique we used in the early days of marketing and marketing research. When we were looking for product benefits to offer customers, we used a technique where we took a person through *every single step* they would take if they were, say, shopping for the product in question. Which store did they go to? Why? Which aisle did they go to? Why? Which shelf did they go to? Why? Where did they look first on the shelf? Did they pick up a product off the shelf?

Did they read the label? What were they looking for on the label? Did they look further on the shelf? And so on.

We are suggesting such an approach to help the millennials and us younger seniors understand what the older ones may be going through in their everyday life. The younger ones can aid older seniors in finding and understanding areas where mobility is seriously compromised.

What Seniors Say They Want

In closing, there is good research from lots of sources on what we seniors look for in selecting a town or city for their retirement. "Close" is the operative word. When asked, seniors want to be close to grocery stores, close to restaurants, and close to walking trails (Real Estate Weekly, 2014).

The online resource Walkable Communities (walkable.org) listed the following in 2005: Walkable neighborhoods. An intact town center with a pleasant main street and a healthy set of stores and shops that are open at least 8 hours per day. A mix of residential densities, mixed income, and mixed use, with higher densities near the town center and in appropriate concentrations further out. Granny flats, design studios, and other affordable housing options. Public spaces to gather, play, and socialize. Universal design. And more. (See also Walkable and Livable Communities Institute.)

So, in closing, the two of us hope that we have provided a few hints here and there to help you make the best of your retirement. Best of luck to all of us in finding and developing a happy future. And now, on with your happy and informed retirement!

About the Authors

Frank and Judy have truly diverse backgrounds. Over their careers, they have gone from being academics to business marketing researchers to entrepreneurs running their own business, to high tech STEM workers, and finally to authors.

As varied as these positions have been, two goals and objectives have always served as the foundation of their work. The first was to use the most advanced methodologies available for working with and understanding consumer and business information. The second was to excel in teaching and communicating their findings to their students and clients. *(Although the term has only recently come into wide use, their field is best known as "big data analytics.")*

Both started their working careers as Assistant Professors at New York University. Frank had just received his Ph.D. in human factors engineering from Cornell University. Judy had received her Ph.D. in quantitative psychology from the University of Colorado. Mid-career saw both Frank and Judy enjoying positions in advertising and marketing research at leading U.S. advertising agencies and corporations.

Both spent a large part of their working years as entrepreneurs, which provided a strong background to their suggestions in the book to start a business. In 1985, Frank started Demand Factors, Inc., an independent marketing research and planning firm. Judy joined him in the business shortly thereafter. The business was heavily involved with organizations working to strengthen America's manufacturing arm and helping to keep jobs in America.

Their last positions took advantage of their high tech backgrounds and again, provided a rich background for the chapters on financing one's retirement and making jobs. Before and after the tech bubble burst, Judy worked as a programmer/analyst and IT project manager. Frank moved to high finance and became a "Quant" at the Bank of America.

They are now in semi-retirement, but keep busy with two websites, http://ourchildrensladder.com/ whose purpose is to help today's kids climb higher in life and http://ludewighouse.com/index.html, the story of their restoration of a Victorian townhouse in St. Louis, Missouri. In preparation is a new website, emphasizing intellectual infrastructure: the machine tools for an information-based economy.

Bibliography

References Cited in the Text plus Additional Readings

Chapter 1

- Fried, C. (2013, May 20). Retirement roadblock: The dangers of magical thinking. *Bloomberg.com*. Retrieved April 30, 2014, from http://www.bloomberg.com/news/2013-05-20/retirement-roadblock-the-dangers-of-magical-thinking-.html

Chapter 2

- Brown, J. (2012, December 12). Downsizing after retirement: should you sell the house and become a renter? *RealEstate.aol.com*. Retrieved April 24, 2014, from http://realestate.aol.com/blog/2012/12/12/downsizing-after-retirement-selling-home-renting/

- Daugherty, G. (2013, May29). Should you rent or buy a home in retirement? *NextAvenue.org*. Retrieved April 23, 2014, from http://www.nextavenue.org/article/2013-05/should-you-rent-or-buy-home-retirement

- Dunleavey, M. (2014, May). Smart or a scam? *Women's Day*, p. 148.

- Hannon, Kerry (2014, June 14). Finding the sweet spot in deciding where to retire. *The New York Times*, p. B4.

- Sightings, T. (2013, August 13). Is it time to sell your house? *U.S. News*. Retrieved April 24, 2014, from http://money.usnews.com/money/blogs/on-retirement/2013/08/13/is-it-time-to-sell-your-house

• Silver-Greenberg, J. (2014, March 27). Inheriting a mortgage pain. *The New York Times*, p. B1.

• Retirement planning – your house. (n.d.). *TheMotleyFool.com*. Retrieved April 24, 2014, from https://www.fool.com/Retirement/RetirementPlanning/retirementplanning09.htm

Chapter 3

• Brandon, E. (2013, October 21). 10 tips for picking a place to retire. *USNews.com*. Retrieved J, 2014, from http://money.usnews.com/money/retirement/articles/2013/10/21/10-tips-for-picking-a-place-to-retire

• Brock, F. (n.d.) Baby boomers' second act. *The New York Times*. Retrieved April 23, 2014, from http://www.nytimes.com/ref/realestate/greathomes/GH-Retire.html

Chapter 4

• 5 things every woman should know about Social Security. (n.d.). *SSA.gov*. Retrieved May 5, 2014 from http://www.ssa.gov/sf/FactSheets/WomenandSSrev1.pdf

• Anderson, N. (2013, June 12). How to retire at 55. *Forbes*. Retrieved April 24, 2014, from http://www.forbes.com/sites/nancyanderson/2013/06/12/how-to-retire-at-55/

• Assisted living costs by geographic location. (n.d.). *SeniorHomes.com*. Retrieved April 24, 2014, from http://www.seniorhomes.com/p/assisted-living-cost/

• Browning, E. S. (2011, February 19). Retiring boomers find 401(k) plans fall short. *Wall Street Journal Online*. Retrieved April 22, 2014, from http://online.wsj.com/news/articles/SB10001424052748703959604576152792748707356#printMode

• Chamberlain, M. (2014, January 27). When should you claim social security benefits? *Forbes*. Retrieved May 5, 2014, from http://www.forbes.com/sites/feeonlyplanner/2014/01/27/when-should-you-claim-social-security-benefits/

• Crawford, M. (2013, November/December). Leveraging state programs to attract relocating retirees. *LeadingAge.org*. Retrieved April 23, 2014, from http://www.leadingage.org/Leveraging_State_Programs_to_Attract_Relocating_Retirees_V3N6.aspx

• Edleson, H. (2014, April 18). Taking a job out of the financial equation. *The New York Times*, p. B1.

• Eisenberg, R. (2013, December 17). Next avenue money score-card: How do you rate? *NextAvenue.org*. Retrieved May 14, 2014 from http://www.nextavenue.org/blog/next-avenue-money-scorecard-how-do-you-rate

• Ellin, A, (2014, February 1). When retirement seems impossible, or just boring. *The New York Times*, p. B4.

• Estimate your retirement income needs. (n.d.). *StateFarm*. Retrieved April 24, 2014, from https://www.statefarm.com/finances/mutual-funds/resources/calculate-your-retirement-income-needs

• Godfrey, H. & Malmgren, E. (2006, July). Going forward with reverse mortgages. *Journal of Accountancy*. Retrieved August 28, 2014 from http://www.journalofaccountancy.com/issues/2006/jul/goingforwardwithreversemortgages.htm

• Hicken, M. (2014, February 13). 401(k) balances hit record $89,300 last year. *CNNMoney*. Retrieved May 14k, 2014 from http://money.cnn.com/2014/02/13/retirement/401k-balances/

• Hicken, M. (2014, June 12). Hidden cost of retiring early: $51,000 in medical bills. *CNNMoney*. Retrieved June 12, 2014 from http://money.cnn.com/2014/06/12/retirement/retirement-health-care/

• How much money will I need in retirement? (n.d.). *CNNMoney*. Retrieved April 24, 2014, from http://money.cnn.com/retirement/guide/basics_basics.moneymag/index5.htm

• Hymowitz, C. (2014, January 2). Baby boomers: poorer in old age than their parents. *Business Week*. Retrieved April 22, 2014, from http://www.businessweek.com/articles/2014-01-02/baby-boomers-poorer-in-old-age-than-their-parents

• Kahn, C. (2013, July 17). Retirement of baby boomers at risk. *Bankrate.com*. Retrieved April 22, 2014, from http://www.bankrate.com/finance/retirement/retirement-baby-boomers-1.aspx

• Keenan, S. (2014, May 8). Grandma never had it so good. *The New York Times*, p. D1.

• Konrad, W. (2014, March 13). Medicare changes prompt enrollees to reconsider plans. *The New York Times*, p. F8.

• Leondis, A (2008, June 13). Reverse mortgages promise seniors cash, advisers urge caution. *Bloomberg.com*. Retrieved August 29, 2014, from http://www.bloomberg.com/apps/news?pid=newsarchive&sid=aN_oIWpG2GqE

• Lynott, W. (2014, October). Managing your money in retirement. *The Elks Magazine*, p. 8.

• Norris, F. (2014, February 7). Ideas to make retirement possible. *The New York Times*, p. B1.

• Phipps, M. (n.d.). Get the money out of your 401(k) or IRA. *Retireplan.About.com*. Retrieved April 24, 2014, from http://retireplan.about.com/od/401kplans/a/Get-The-Money-Out-Of-Your-401-K-Or-Ira.htm

• Principle 2: Develop a suitable asset allocation using broadly diversified funds. (n.d.). *Vanguard.com*. Retrieved April 24, 2014, from https://personal.vanguard.com/us/insights/investingtruths/investing-truth-about-risk

• Retiree health costs fall. (2013, May 15). *Fidelity*. Retrieved May 14, 2014 from https://www.fidelity.com/viewpoints/retirement/retirees-medical-expenses

• Riley, C. (2012, June 12). Family net worth plummets nearly 40%. *CNNMoney*. Retrieved May 5, 2014, from http://money.cnn.com/2012/06/11/news/economy/fed-family-net-worth/

• Steiner, S. (2009, October 6). Americans plan to work through retirement. *Bankrate.com*. Retrieved April 22, 2014, from http://www.bankrate.com/finance/financial-literacy/americans-plan-to-work-through-retirement-1.aspx

• The 4% Rule: The easy answer to "how much do I need for retirement?" (May 29, 2012). *MrMoneyMustache.com*. Retrieved May 5, 2014 from http://www.mrmoneymustache.com/2012/05/29/how-much-do-i-need-for-retirement/

• Top 10 ways to prepare for retirement (n.d.). *United States Department of Labor*. Retrieved September 3, 2014, from http://www.dol.gov/ebsa/publications/10_ways_to_prepare.html

• Use reverse mortgages with caution (n.d.). *Investor Solutions.com*. Retrieved August 29, 2014, from http://investorsolutions.com/knowledge-center/personal-finance/use-reverse-mortgages-with-caution/

• Waggoner, J. (2013, October 21). 3%? 4%? 5%? How much to take for retirement. *USA Today*. Retrieved February 10, 2014 from http://www.usatoday.com/story/money/columnist/waggoner/2013/07/18/retirement-savings-withdrawals/2552669/

• Waggoner, J. (2014, May 3). Social security can be a waiting game. *USA Today for Fort Collins Coloradean,* p.5B.

• Working after retirement: the gap between expectations and reality. (2006, September 21). *PewSocialTrends.org*. Retrieved February 6, 2014, from http://www.pewsocialtrends.org/2006/09/21/working-after-retirement-the-gap-between-expectations-and-reality/

• Zimmerman, E. (2013, May 14). 4% rule for retirement withdrawals is golden no more. *The New York Times*. Retrieved April 24, 2014, from http://www.nytimes.com/2013/05/15/business/retirementspecial/the-4-rule-for-retirement-withdrawals-may-be-outdated.html?_r=0

Chapter 5

• Browning, E. S. (2011, February 19). Retiring boomers find 401(k) plans fall short. *Wall Street Journal Online*. Retrieved April 30, 2014, from http://online.wsj.com/news/articles/SB10001424052748703959604576152792748707356

• Carrns, A. (2014, March 1). Save for retirement first, the children's education second. *The New York Times*, p. B4.

• DeBare, I. (n.d.). Keeping a packed bag at work: employees today are more apt to job hop than ever before. *San Francisco Chronicle*. Retrieved May 13, 2014 from http://www.sfgate.com/business/article/Keeping-A-Packed-Bag-at-Work-Employees-today-2933410.php

• Greenhouse, S. (2014, March 13). The gray jobs enigma. *The New York Times*, p. F1.

• Health Insurance Portability and Accountability Act. (n.d.) *Wikipedia.* Retrieved May 14k, 2014 from http://en.wikipedia.org/wiki/Health_Insurance_Portability_and_Accountability_Act

• Krugman, Paul (2014, February 10). Writing off the unemployed. *The New York Times*, p. A19.

• Laura, R. (2013, September 30). The real reason why baby boomers are so far behind in retirement savings. *Forbes*. Retrieved April 22, 2014, from http://www.forbes.com/sites/robertlaura/2013/09/30/the-real-reason-why-baby-boomers-are-so-far-behind-in-retirement-savings/

• O'Connell, B. (2013, February 7). Your happy retirement is probably about $250,000 short. *YahooFinance.com*. Retrieved February 10, 2014, from http://finance.yahoo.com/news/happy-retirement-probably-250-000-192800412.html

• RealtyTrac: 9.1 million homes still seriously under water (April 17, 2014). *MortgageOrb.com*. Retrieved April 30, 2014, from http://www.mortgageorb.com/e107_plugins/content/content.php?content.15719/

• Repa, B. (n.d.). Many employees still have some form of pension plan, although they aren't as common as they used to be. *Nolo*. Retrieved May 13, 2014 from http://www.nolo.com/legal-encyclopedia/free-books/employee-rights-book/chapter14-3.html

• Tankersley, J. (2012, October 5). Who destroyed the economy? The case against the baby boomers. *The Atlantic*. Retrieved April 25, 2014, from http://www.theatlantic.com/business/archive/2012/10/who-destroyed-the-economy-the-case-against-the-baby-boomers/263291/

• There are 3 unemployed people for every job opening, Obama advisor says (n.d.). P*olitifact.com*. Retrieved April 30, 2014, from http://www.politifact.com/truth-o-meter/statements/2014/jan/07/gene-sperling/there-are-3-unemployed-people-every-job-opening-ob/

• Walsh, M. (November 11, 2014). Detroit emerges from bankruptcy yet pension risks linger. *New York Times*. Retrieved November 11, 2014, from http://dealbook.nytimes.com/2014/11/11/detroit-emerges-from-bankruptcy-pension-risk-still-intact/?_r=0

• What is Rule of 85 retirement? (n.d.). *ask.com*. Retrieved May 14, 2014, from http://www.ask.com/question/what-is-rule-of-85-retirement

• Wimbish, K. (2012, January 19). Nearly 70% of American workers will fund their own retirement. *Wells Fargo*. Retrieved April 19, 2012, from http://wellsfargo.com/retirement/2012/01/nearly-70-of-american-workers-will-fund-their-own-retirement/

Chapter 6

- Ashford, K. (2013, November). The real cost of care. *Woman's Day*, p. 37.

- Ellin, A. (2014, February 15). The childless plan for their fading days. *The New York Times*, p. B4.

- Kelly, C. (2013, May 14). Covering the rising cost of long term care. *The New York Times*. Retrieved April 23, 2014, from http://www.nytimes.com/2013/05/15/business/retirementspecial/covering-the-rising-cost-of-long-term-care.html?_r=0

- Manjoo, F. (2014, February 2014). How to survive the next wave of technology extinction. *The New York Times*, p. B1.

Chapter 7

- Aging-in-Place remodeling checklist (n.d.). National Association of Home Builders. Retrieved August 10, 2014 from http://www.nahb.org/generic.aspx?genericContentID=89801

- Bawden, D. (n.d.). What is design for independent living anyway? *NAHB.org*. Retrieved April 25, 2014, from http://www.nahb.org/generic.aspx?sectionID=717&genericContentID=114505

- Leibrock, C. (n.d.). The secrets to aging beautifully. *Aging-Beautifully.org*. Retrieved April 25, 2014, from http://www.agingbeautifully.org/ranch.html

- Tenenbaum, L. (2013, July 25). 8 things to consider before remodeling to age in place. *NextAvenue.org.*. Retrieved April 25, 2014 from http://www.nextavenue.org/article/2013-07/8-things-consider-remodeling-age-place

- What Is universal design? (2009. September 30). *AARP.org*. Retrieved April 25, 2014, from http://www.aarp.org/home-garden/home-improvement/info-09-2009/what_is_universal_design.print.html

Chapter 8

• 10 things baby boomers won't tell you. (2013, July 17). *Marketwatch.com*. Retrieved April 23, 2014, from http://www.marketwatch.com/story/10-things-boomers-wont-tell-you-2013-07-12?pagenumber=1

• Brody, J. (2011, February 22). Tackling care as chronic ailments pile up. *The New York Times*. Retrieved June 12, 2014 from http://www.nytimes.com/2011/02/22/health/22brody.html?_r=0

• Brody, J. (2014, March 4). The perils of toughing it out. *The New York Times*, p. D7.

• Carrns, A. (2013, November 20). You plan your retirement, then you get the health bill. *The New York Times*, p. F1.

• Fell, J. (2012, January 16). In-your-face fitness: go ahead, run into old age. *Los Angeles Times*. Retrieved April 22, 2014, from http://articles.latimes.com/2012/jan/16/health/la-he-fitness-running-joints-20120116

• Retiree health costs fall. (2013, May 15). *Fidelity*. Retrieved May 14, 2014 from https://www.fidelity.com/viewpoints/retirement/retirees-medical-expenses

• What to do if you have multiple medical problems. (n.d.). *University of Kentucky Healthcare*. Retrieved June 12, 2014 from http://ukhealthcare.uky.edu/publications/healthsmart/multiple-medical-problems/

Chapter 9

• Anderson, J., & Esswein, P. (2013, May). Declutter your life. *Kiplinger.com*. Retrieved April 23, 2014, from http://www.kiplinger.com/article/real-estate/T065-C000-S000-declutter-your-life.html

• Hawthorne, F. (2014, February 11). When boomers inherit, complications may follow. *The New York Times*, p. F6.

• How long to keep important papers (n.d.). *GoodHousekeeping.com*. Retrieved September 4, 2014 from http://www.goodhousekeeping.com/home/cleaning-organizing/important-papers-to-keep

• Managing household records (2014, July 17). *USA.gov*. Retrieved September 4, 2014 from http://www.usa.gov/Topics/Money/Personal-Finance/Managing-Household-Records.shtml

• Schillinger, L. (2014, April 20). A formal setting. *The New York Times Magazine*, p. 50.

• Wallis, L. (2014, February). Order in the house. *Family Circle*, p. 23.

• What does a professional organizer do? (n.d.). *Cluttersort.com*. Retrieved April 23, 2014, from http://www.cluttersort.com/

Chapter 10

• Carey, B. (2014, January 28). Older mind may just be a fuller mind. *The New York Times*, p. D3.

• Knapton, S. (2014, January 20). Brains of elderly slow because they know so much. *The Telegraph*. Retrieved April 23, 2014, from http://www.telegraph.co.uk/science/science-news/10584927/Brains-of-elderly-slow-because-they-know-so-much.html

• Korkki, P. (2014, March 13). The science of older and wiser. *The New York Times*, p. F1.

• Lazar, Kay (2014, January 13). Study finds long-lasting results from brain exercises. *The Boston Globe*. Retrieved April 22, 2014, from http://www.bostonglobe.com/lifestyle/health-wellness/2014/01/13/brain-training-can-help-older-adults-stave-off-aging-impairments-study-finds/QTrB2E6UsXB8hYIeMvbJII/story.html.

Chapter 11

• Bernard, D. (2012, June 22). 3 necessities for a happy retirement. *US News*. Retrieved April 23, 2014, from http://money.usnews.com/money/blogs/on-retirement/2012/06/22/3-necessities-for-a-happy-retirement

• Tanner, L. (2014, March 14). Explore artsy Asheville, N.C. for free. *Fort Collins Coloradean*, p. C3.

Chapter 12

• Dreifus, C. (2014, January 28). It all started with a 12-year-old cousin. *The New York Times*, p. D5.

• Dubner, S.J. (2013, May 1). It's crowded at the top: a new marketplace podcast. *Freakonomics.com*. Retrieved March 3, 2014, from http://freakonomics.com/2013/05/01/its-crowded-at-the-top-a-new-marketplace-podcast/

• Hannon, K. (2014, February 8). For many older Americans, an entrepreneurial path. *The New York Times,* p.B4.

• Hannon, K. (2014, March 8). An aging population also poses opportunities for retirement careers. *The New York Times*, p. B7.

• Hutchins, G. (2014, March 15). Work like a German. *The New York Times*, p. A19.

• Krugman, P. (014, March 31). Jobs and skills and zombies. *The New York Times*, p. A19

• Lauricella, T. (2013, November 3). Five things you think you know about retirement. *Wall Street Journal Sunday*, p. WSJ-2.

• Richtel, M. (2014, May 11). Reading, writing, arithmetic, and now coding. *The New York Times*, p. A1.

• Singer, N. (2014, August 17). Check App. Accept Job. Repeat. *The New York Times, Sunday Business*, p.1.

PostScript

• Aronson, L. (2014, November 2). New buildings for older people. *The New York Times*, p. 4.

• Edleson, H. (2014, October 18). When planning for retirement, consider transportation. *The New York Times*, p. B4.

• Ewing, S. (2014, August 16). Generation gap appears to fade away when it comes to community amenities. *Real Estate Weekly*, p. 6.

• What makes a community walkable? Retrieved January 6, 2015, from http://walkablestreets.wordpress.com/2005/08/18/principles-of-walkable-communities/

www.ingramcontent.com/pod-product-compliance
Lightning Source LLC
Chambersburg PA
CBHW060034210326
41520CB00009B/1124